Enhancing Student Learning
Intellectual, Social, and Emotional Integration

by Patrick G. Love and Anne Goodsell Love

ASHE-ERIC Higher Education Report No. 4, 1995

Prepared by

Clearinghouse on Higher Education
The George Washington University

In cooperation with

Association for the Study
of Higher Education

Published by

Graduate School of Education and Human Development
The George Washington University

Jonathan D. Fife, Series Editor

Cite as
Love, Patrick G., and Anne Goodsell Love. 1995. *Enhancing Student Learning: Intellectual, Social, and Emotional Integration*. ASHE-ERIC Higher Education Report No. 4. Washington, D.C.: The George Washington University, Graduate School of Education and Human Development.

Library of Congress Catalog Card Number 96-77446
ISSN 0884-0040
ISBN 1-878380-68-0

Managing Editor: Lynne J. Scott
Manuscript Editor: Alexandra Rockey
Cover Design by Michael David Brown, Rockville, Maryland

The ERIC Clearinghouse on Higher Educaton invites individuals to submit proposals for writing monographs for the *ASHE-ERIC Higher Education Report* series. Proposals must include:
1. A detailed manuscript proposal of not more than five pages.
2. A chapter-by-chapter outline.
3. A 75-word summary to be used by several review committees for the initial screening and rating of each proposal.
4. A vita and a writing sample.

ERIC **Clearinghouse on Higher Education**
Graduate School of Education and Human Development
The George Washington University
One Dupont Circle, Suite 630
Washington, DC 20036-1183

This publication was prepared partially with funding from the Office of Education Research and Improvement, U.S. Department of Education, under contract no. ED RR-93-002008. The opinions expressed in this report do not necessarily reflect the positions or policies of OERI or the Department.

EXECUTIVE SUMMARY

The need to focus on holistic learning—the integration of intellectual, social, and emotional aspects of undergraduate student learning—has been voiced periodically throughout the last half-century (American Council on Education 1949; Boyer 1987; Brown 1972; Miller and Prince 1976; Williamson 1957). Recent research on student experience and college impact has provided additional fuel to these arguments (Astin 1984, 1993; Pascarella and Terenzini 1991; Springer et al. 1995; Tinto 1993, for example). The roles of faculty and student affairs professionals have become so disparate that neither focus on student learning to their fullest extent. Each focuses on a part of the whole, but in so doing students' education becomes only the sum of its parts, not more.

Furthermore, higher education has struggled for a long time with the increasing fragmentation of the learning process, of disciplines and knowledge, of the administrative structure, and of community. Strong cultural forces have acted as barriers to efforts at reforming and transforming higher education, but now forces within and out of higher education have gathered that are exerting tremendous pressure on the entire enterprise. These include the growing body of research linking intellectual, social, and emotional processes, a continuing paradigm shift in the social sciences and education, the emergence of disciplines that incorporate the impact of social processes and issues of affect (women's studies; pan-African studies; gay, lesbian, and bisexual studies), continuing reform efforts (total quality management, general education, and core curriculum reemergence), and external pressures (the accountability movement, mandated outcomes assessment, and financial cutbacks at the state and federal levels). The need for reform is clear.

What does research say about the relationship among the intellectual, social, and emotional elements of student learning?

Traditional literature regarding college students' intellectual, social, and emotional development is dominated by three underlying assumptions: student affairs professionals deal solely with social and emotional development; faculty deal solely with intellectual development; and the ways to integrate intellectual, social and emotional development are by linking in-class and out-of-class experiences and by linking student affairs professionals and faculty. This report views the intellectual, social, and emotional divide from a broader and more inclusive perspective which recognizes that student learning can and should be integrated in additional ways.

A growing literature base reinforces the fact that cognitive*, social, and emotional processes are inextricably linked. For example, recent theories of cognitive development, especially Baxter Magolda (1992, 1995), Belenky et al. (1986), and Gilligan (1982), clearly acknowledge the role played by social context and interpersonal relationships. It also is recognized that learning is facilitated or hampered by emotions (Boekaerts 1993; Goleman 1995), that emotions drive learning and memory (Sylvester 1994), and that depressed mood states often correlate with decreased motivation in the classroom (Peterson and Seligman 1984).

What can individual faculty and student affairs professionals do to enhance holistic learning?

Traditional educational practices, especially teaching pedagogies that reflect the dominance of and reliance on lecture as the sole method of classroom instruction, clearly are under attack (Freire 1978; Giroux 1983; Schniedewind and Davidson 1987). In their place have proliferated such interrelated philosophies, pedagogies, and practices as liberation theory (Freire 1970; McClaren and Leonard 1993; Shor 1992), constructivist pedagogy (Brooks and Brooks 1993), adopting a critical cultural perspective (Rhoads and Black 1995), and collaborative learning (Bruffee 1987, 1993; Gabelnick et al. 1990; Goodsell et al. 1992). These practices challenge the traditional models of teaching and learning because they acknowledge, address, and make use of social and emotional influences on learning. By changing the nature of authority in learning experiences or by bringing the personal experiences of students to bear on a topic, these practices hold tremendous potential for reshaping individual practice and, in turn, higher education.

A basic premise of liberation theory is that society's cultural system perpetuates power relationships and holds people (and groups) in place like an invisible web (Freire 1970). Freire argued that the educational system must be transformed through praxis, which is "reflection and action

---

*Throughout this report we use three sets of interchangeable terms: cognitive and intellectual, social and interpersonal, and emotional and affective.

upon the world in order to transform it" (Freire 1970, p. 36). Constructivist pedagogy is based on the premise that teachers "must provide a learning environment where students search for meaning, appreciate uncertainty, and inquire responsibly" (Jackson 1993, p. v). It recognizes that emphasis on performance and giving the right answers results in little long-term recall, whereas a focus on learning results in greater long-term understanding and ability to use the concepts and information out of the classroom (Katz 1985). Constructivist pedagogy helps students "to take responsibility for their own learning, to be autonomous thinkers, to develop integrated understandings of concepts, and to pose—and seek to answer—important questions" (Brooks and Brooks 1993, p. 13).

Similarly, adopting a critical cultural perspective recognizes the strength and embeddedness of the current culture and subcultures (Rhoads and Black 1995). This perspective requires that the underlying assumptions of our current system of higher education be identified, analyzed, and changed if effective and lasting change is to occur regarding student learning. Educators—both faculty and student affairs professionals—must examine their assumptions and values, as well as how they are put into practice.

Collaborative learning strategies enhance learning by actively incorporating social and affective dynamics between students and between students and faculty. Such strategies are based upon the idea that acquiring and creating knowledge is an active social process students need to practice; it is not a process in which students are spectators sitting passively in a lecture hall (Bruffee 1984, 1993).

What can institutions do to enhance holistic learning?
Implications for institutions moving toward developing an ethos of holistic learning include providing visionary, persistent, and pervasive leadership; promoting student involvement in learning; developing learning communities; enhancing the educational climate of residence halls; and intentionally influencing the socialization of faculty and student affairs professionals.

Persistent leadership is required because cultures themselves are quite persistent (Kuh 1993a; Schein 1985), and pervasive leadership implies both that the leadership of the institution must be seen as pervading the institution and that multiple leaders supporting and pushing the transformation must come from throughout the institution and its hierarchy. Methods to promote student involvement include expanding the number of leadership roles on campus, creating environments and situations in which all students have opportunities to participate and contribute, fostering and rewarding student-initiated opportunities, and providing formal and informal awards for involvement (Kuh, Schuh, and Whitt 1991).

The development of learning communities requires collaboration between traditional faculty and student affairs areas and, in doing so, breaks down many of the barriers to enhancing students' holistic learning. Students in learning communities provide social, emotional, and intellectual support for each other's learning, and learning communities are ideal places in which faculty members may implement collaborative learning strategies.

Institutions also must pay closer attention to the cultural socialization and orientation of its members. Institutions can influence the socialization of faculty and student affairs professionals through teaching-assistant training programs, student affairs graduate preparation programs, and ongoing professional staff training.

CONTENTS

FOREWORD

Over the years, as clearly described in this report, a significant body of research has given evidence to the impact of colleges on students when there is a clear integration of intellectual, emotional, and social development. In the integrative studies by both Feldman and Newcomb (1969) and Terenzini and Pascarella (1991) the conclusions were the same: Those institutions that carefully choreographed cognitive or intellectual development with the affective or emotional development and the interpersonal or social development had the greatest impact on their students.

There are a number of reasons why the environment of higher education institutions, especially the larger institutions, have perpetuated a separation of the intellectual development objectives from the emotional and social development objectives. Significantly contributing to this division are:

- *Organizational structure:* Over the years, most institutions have separated the academic, teaching and research activities from the out-of-classroom experiences. The former are responsible to the provost or vice president for academic affairs; the latter to the vice president for student affairs. Rarely do these two distinct organizational areas meet to discuss their mutual interests in the total education of the students. This separation is compounded by a separate business affairs staff that often manages the financial resources of the institution in a separate context than the education mission of both academic affairs and student affairs.
- *Lack of training:* Academic, student, and business professionals have one thing in common. They have received limited formal or on-the-job education concerning the developmental theories that underlie areas other than their own. As a result of this lack of training, an insensitivity to the importance that different areas have for fulfilling the education mission of the institution may develop and result in an inability to work together in an integrative process.
- *Lack of communication:* In some institutions, there is a lack of sensitivity and understanding of the importance of integrating intellectual, emotional, and social development. Institutions have not formed a communication system that will promote continuous discussions concerning ways that each area could support the others.

- *Lack of professional incentives:* For most institutions, the overall reward system, which includes both positive and negative reinforcements, does not have incentives that promote strong, collaborative effort in bringing together the three developmental areas. In a culture that values specialization, the responsibility to promote change increasingly rests with the overall leadership of the institution.

There are a number of reasons why institutions should make it part of their mission to develop a more comprehensive or integrative approach to their education process.

- *Increased educational impact on students:* The research on student learning and on the institutions that have the greatest impact on their students demonstrate that there is an interrelationship and interdependency in the intellectual, emotional, and social development of students. The more efforts that are made to get students actively and emotionally involved in their academic program and to relate their academic program to outside the classroom, the greater is the overall intellectual achievement of the student.
- *Increased student retention:* A second and very important result to both institutions and students is that the greater the integration of these developmental areas, the more strongly students are motivated to complete their studies. When the academic area is more closely linked with overall life objectives and when there is a greater interrelationship between the academic and social aspects of a college education, the more likely students will pursue their degree program to completion.
- *Greater social harmony:* When students are actively emotionally, socially, and intellectually engaged with both their academic program and each other, there develops a greater understanding and sensitivity for individual similarities and differences. The amount of ethnic and gender discord frequently witnessed on the larger college campuses are seen far less frequently on those campuses that have developed a more integrated student developmental process.
- *Decreased social deviations:* There also is a decrease in deviant social behavior such as drug and alcohol abuse

when students develop a stronger sense of self that occurs with an integrated developmental process.

This report by Patrick G. Love, professor of higher education and student personnel at Kent State University, and Anne Goodsell Love, assistant to the vice president of student affairs at The University of Akron, comprehensively examines the integration of intellectual, social, and emotional student development. The authors pay particular attention to both findings of research and the relationship and interdependency of these developmental areas as well as examining theoretical models that this research has supported. Based upon this careful review, the authors conclude their report by examining the implications to faculty and student affairs professionals and for the institution as a whole.

Love and Goodsell Love have developed a report that will be very useful to institutions that look to develop a more comprehensive approach in their education mission. What is presented here will help develop a common understanding between the academic and student affairs disciplines promoting increased communication and mutual respect for the contributions each professional segment makes to the integration of these developmental areas into the education mission. As this communication process develops, this report also will be useful in helping to create new ways of examining developmental issues and how they can contribute to making intellectual, emotional, and social education objectives a mutual responsibility and a fundamental part of the institution's culture.

Jonathan D. Fife
Series Editor,
Professor of Higher Education Administration and
Director, ERIC Clearinghouse on Higher Education

ACKNOWLEDGMENTS

We would like to thank a number of people who have been generous in their support and encouragement of our work. The mentorship of Don Hossler, George Kuh, and Vincent Tinto profoundly influenced both of us, and without their guidance along the way we would not be writing about the topic of this report. Other colleagues who have contributed to our understanding include Pat Russo, Dan Tompkins, Nancy Hoffman, and Kathy Manning. We also acknowledge the support of Caryl Kelley Smith and thank Myrna Villanueva for her help in spending many hours in finding and copying sources.

Special thanks go to colleagues who reviewed drafts of this report: Sandy Estanek, Marlene Dorsey, Lee Williams, Carol Van Der Karr, and Michael Poock. We also appreciate the comments and critiques offered by anonymous colleagues.

INTRODUCTION

The history of higher education in the United States is one in which the intellectual, social, and emotional processes of college students' experience have grown increasingly segregated. In colonial colleges, even though the president and faculty were focused solely on intellectual and moral development, the fact that colleges were small, residential communities and this small group of individuals was responsible for students' experience contributed to the possibility of holistic learning on the part of students.

During this century, however, institutions of higher education have continued to shift their focus primarily to intellectual development, relinquishing students' social and emotional development to other professionals and to the students themselves. Faculty were finding that time devoted to their scholarship was increasingly rewarded over time spent in activities such as student advising. They retreated to their offices, classrooms, and labs, and they also retreated from a sense of commitment to students' nonintellectual experiences and development. The faculty, however, were not alone in this emerging scenario. Students were as active a force in bringing about this change as faculty, devoting much time to campus activities, athletics, and their social lives (Horowitz 1987). Students increasingly differentiated life in the classroom from life beyond the classroom and intellectual development from the personal issues of social and emotional development (Feldman and Newcomb 1969). For many campuses, this trend may be accelerating in the 1990s, as growing numbers of students work full time or part time, take classes part time, and have family responsibilities that draw them away from the life of the campus.

The field of student affairs emerged and grew steadily at the turn of the 20th century as the trend for faculty research accelerated and the numbers of students at institutions increased. Student affairs professionals focused on social and emotional development by stepping into the void left by the faculty. Although some needs of the students were being met by student affairs professionals filling this void, it also served to continue to divide social, emotional, and intellectual processes. A student affairs professional organization noted in 1975 the differing missions of faculty and student affairs professionals, stating that "in general, faculty tend to emphasize content and student development specialists tend to emphasize process" (Council of Student Personnel

The history of higher education in the United States is one in which the intellectual, social, and emotional processes of college students' experience have grown increasingly segregated.

Associations in Higher Education 1975, p. 3). Derek Bok, former Harvard University president, described it by suggesting, "Professors . . . are trained to transmit knowledge and skills, not to help students become more mature, morally perceptive human beings" (1988, p. B4).

The need to integrate the intellectual, social, and emotional aspects of undergraduate student learning in higher education has been voiced periodically throughout the last half-century (American Council on Education 1949; Boyer 1987; Brown 1972; Miller and Prince 1976; Williamson 1957) and has led to some attempts to bridge this gap on particular campuses (Goodsell 1993; Roueche and Baker 1987). Recent research on students' experiences and the impact of college on students has provided additional fuel to the argument that better efforts to integrate students' social, emotional, and intellectual development must be made throughout academe (e.g., Astin 1984, 1993; Pascarella and Terenzini 1991; Springer et al. 1995; Tinto 1993). This argument is not made because anyone wants to revert to patterns of the past for reasons of nostalgia, but because both faculty and student affairs professionals have become removed from the primary mission of higher education—namely, to educate the whole student. The roles of faculty and student affairs professionals have become so disparate that neither focus to their fullest extent on student learning. Each focuses on a part of the whole, but in so doing, students' education becomes only the sum of its parts, not more. The integrative experiences required to apply knowledge to moral or social ends remain undervalued and unaddressed (Cross 1976).

A Contradiction Between Knowledge and Behavior

Part of the recent history of the segregation of the intellectual, social, and emotional processes of learning is a contradiction that exists between what we in higher education know to be true about student learning and our actions related to student learning. The segregation of intellectual, emotional, and social aspects of student learning takes place in a higher-education culture—and, especially, a student affairs culture—which believes feelings affect thinking and learning (Lyons 1990; National Association of Student Personnel Administrators 1987). As is delineated in this report, a growing body of research supports this belief. Additionally, there is widespread acceptance and research evidence to support Tinto's assertions regarding the link between social integration in college and student retention and success (1993). Consequently, few would argue that social processes, in and out of the classroom, do not have an important influence on student learning. Furthermore, research repeatedly has shown that out-of-class experiences have a substantial impact on college students—intellectually, emotionally, socially, morally, physically, and mentally (Boyer 1987; Kuh, Schuh, and Whitt 1991; Miller and Jones 1981), and that faculty have a role to play in a student's overall college experience and development (Gaff and Gaff 1981; Pascarella and Terenzini 1981, 1991).

Our practices and their underlying assumptions, however, belie these truths. Members of the higher-education community know that the intellectual, social, and emotional aspects of students' education should be integrated throughout their educational experience to enhance their overall development. These same members also know that such integration does not commonly happen, in part because this segregated arrangement is beneficial to both faculty and student affairs professionals. Faculty have benefited from their sole focus on intellectual activity which, in turn, has allowed a focus on research and scholarship. And although the claim has been made that student affairs professionals are focused on holistic student development—that it is their *raison d'etre* (Kuh, Shedd, and Whitt 1987)—it must be recognized that they, in fact, have focused primarily on social, emotional, and moral development, often ignoring intellectual and cognitive development (Kuh, Bean, Bradley, and Coomes 1986). There is much activity in student affairs surrounding *The Student Learning Imperative*, which calls for a greater emphasis on student learning by student affairs professionals (American College Personnel Association 1994). This activity includes a special issue of the *Journal of College Student Development* (March/April 1996), a national conference theme on student learning (National Association of Student Personnel Administrators, March 1996), a listserv devoted to discussion of the topic, and a forthcoming National Association of Student Personnel Administrators monograph, *Redefining Learning*. This recent call for a greater emphasis by student affairs professionals on student learning gives further credence to the claim that in the past student affairs professionals have been concerned primarily about social and emotional development.

The activities and behaviors of both faculty and student affairs professionals are supported by the cultures that have developed within academe. Both cultures contradict what they know to be true by continuing to segregate intellectual development from social and emotional processes. The long history and strength of these cultures make the situation increasingly resistant to change. This brings us to the topic of this report—an examination of the history, current conditions, initiatives, strategies, and implications for integrating the intellectual, social, and emotional aspects of student learning. We synthesize literature from a number of areas of research that are instrumental in understanding how the integration of the intellectual, social, and emotional elements of student learning can be facilitated more effectively at colleges and universities.

A Focus on How to Integrate

The literature that forms the foundation of this report focuses primarily on how, rather than whether, the intellectual, social, and emotional aspects of college students' learning should be integrated. Much of the current literature addressing the issue of how to more holistically address student learning reflects two divergent themes. Student affairs practitioners, on one side, urge faculty and administrators to take seriously the role that student affairs plays in students' social, affective, and moral development. This literature exhorts student affairs professionals to make contact with faculty and academic-affairs administrators and to lure faculty out of their classrooms, thereby bringing intellectual development out of the classroom (e.g., Mitchell and Roof 1989; Reger and Hyman 1988; Schroeder, DiTiberio, and Kalsbeek 1988; Stringer, Steckler, and Johnson 1988). The operating assumption is that faculty members are the only agents of intellectual development on campus.

On the other side, the literature consists of researchers and faculty focusing their efforts, for the most part, on students' intellectual and cognitive development. When research does examine social or emotional processes, they often are examined in isolation. As Polkosnik and Winston point out: "There has been significant effort devoted to the study of cognitive and psychosocial development as separate processes; little work has been directed toward gaining an understanding of the integration of these sub-processes in the individual" (1989, p. 11). Both sides talk past each other in that they write for different audiences, are members of different professional organizations, and are stymied by forces much larger than themselves—the cultural milieu of higher education (Kuh and Whitt 1988; Tierney and Rhoads 1994)—when they try to bridge the gap in these traditional ways.

These divergent literature bases have three underlying assumptions: 1) student affairs professionals deal solely with social and emotional development; 2) faculty deal solely with intellectual development; and 3) the ways to reintegrate intellectual, social, and emotional development are by linking in-class and out-of-class experiences and by linking student affairs professionals and faculty. Neither group (faculty or student affairs professionals) is assumed to have the expertise and neither location (in or out of class) is assumed to provide the environment needed to enhance all three aspects of development simultaneously. These perspectives ultimately are incomplete and limiting.

We see the intellectual, social, and emotional divide from a broader and more inclusive perspective. This perspective recognizes that holistic learning can be facilitated both in the classroom by faculty and out of the classroom by student affairs professionals. The traditional paradigm of intellectual, social, and emotional development, as reflected in the literature referred to previously, designates intellectual development as the domain of the faculty and assumes that it happens only in class (or in classlike conditions). In a similar manner, the traditional paradigm views social and emotional development as the purview of student affairs professionals and assumes that these processes of development happen out of class. The more inclusive perspective that forms the organizing framework of this report recognizes that the intellectual, social, and emotional aspects of learning can be integrated in additional ways. More important, by connecting cognitive, social, and emotional processes and bringing them to bear on the process of student learning, student learning ultimately is enhanced.

This perspective, which focuses on intellectual development by recognizing the catalytic function of emotional and social processes, recognizes that integrating all three can be brought about by faculty in the classroom. Equally so, intellectual, social, and emotional integration can be brought about by student affairs professionals working out of the classroom. The strict division of labor between faculty (intellectual development) and student affairs (social and emotional development) can be softened with the increasing realization that intellectual development does not happen exclusively in class and that social and emotional development do not happen exclusively out of class. The further realization must be made that to focus exclusively on only one aspect of development is to miss the greater benefits that each contributes to the other.

This perspective, then, enables us to incorporate the research and literature that describe programs and pedagogies incorporating emotional and social processes and development in and through classes, such as learning communities and collaborative learning strategies (e.g., Gablenick et al. 1990; Tinto et al. 1993). This perspective also incorporates programs that bring academic concerns and intellectual development to out-of-class experiences, such as living-learning centers (e.g., Chickering and Reisser 1993; Forrest 1985; Pascarella and Terenzini 1981, 1991). In addition, this perspective is made possible by the inclusion of literature that explores pedagogies that are alternatives to the traditional lecture format, such as liberation theory (Freire 1970; Shor 1992) and constructivist pedagogy (Brooks and Brooks 1993). This report not only addresses the issue of integrating students' intellectual, social, and emotional development, but it also provides an opportunity to bridge the literature bases that have developed around exploring and promoting social and emotional development in the classroom and integrating intellectual, social, and emotional development outside the classroom.

Terminology

We have chosen to use the term *holistic student learning* to reflect both an emphasis on the intellectual dimension of students' educational experience and a conscious recognition that learning takes place in the context of social processes and emotional influences. It also recognizes the concurrent nature of development in the cognitive, social, and affective realms of students' lives. In this report we include cognitive development and content learning within the broader rubric of intellectual development. Although at times used synonymously, we recognize distinctions between social processes and social development and emotional influences and emotional development. Given our emphasis on holistic student learning, we concentrate on the role of intellectual, social, and emotional processes in facilitating this learning. We assert, however, that by focusing on social and emotional aspects of learning, higher-education professionals also will be enhancing social and emotional development.

Social processes refer to the range of interpersonal interactions between students and their peers, the faculty, and other campus professionals. Our use of the term *social development* goes beyond processes and includes such constructs as the development of autonomy, interdependence, mature interpersonal relationships, identity, and purpose (Chickering and Reisser 1993). Throughout this report we have separated emotional development and emotional influences from social development and processes. Emotional influences include internal affective states such as interest, motivation, curiosity, and stress, and emotions such as depression, joy, happiness, anger, love, hope, and other positive and negative feeling states. Emotional development refers to the process through which students become aware of emotions and their influence (Goleman 1995), learn to manage these various states (Chickering and Reisser 1993), and incorporate them into their overall development.

Many people in the field of higher education refer to academic development and usually equate it with intellectual or cognitive development. This use implies that everything academic is intellectual. As we point out later in the report, the tendency to think of academic development only in intellectual or cognitive terms serves to emphasize the dichotomy that exists between social and emotional development and the development of intellectual skills. Furthermore, we describe research that supports the interrelatedness of intellectual, social, and emotional processes and development. Social, emotional, physical, moral, and ethical development all are possible within academe; the effectiveness with which they are fostered is a different story. But because the term *academic development* can be misinterpreted so easily, we avoid its use.

Integration and Its Implications

Integrating the intellectual, social, and emotional processes of student learning requires more than exhortation. It requires an understanding of both the barriers that prevent the integration and the conditions that have developed to support the uniting of these elements. Integration also requires strategies to overcome the barriers and tactics to support and extend the facilitating conditions. Only then can we effectively disseminate throughout higher education the research, programs, and other strategies that have begun to bridge this divide.

In this report we identify current cultural barriers to integrating intellectual, social, and emotional development on college and university campuses. We also identify those circumstances, issues, and changes that are helping to create conditions in which intellectual, social, and emotional development more easily might be integrated, such as an expanding literature base linking intellectual, social, and emotional processes, external pressures (Shaffer 1993), and a continuing paradigm shift in higher education toward transforming the curriculum. These facilitating conditions are helpful but insufficient in and of themselves to accomplish the task of integrating students' development.

The centerpiece of this report is the identification of models, strategies, and implications that will be useful to a wide audience concerned with integrating the intellectual, social, and emotional aspects of students' development. We focus first on the actions individual educators (i.e., faculty and student affairs professionals) can take to transform their own practice to one through which the intellectual, social, and emotional elements of learning are integrated. Individual reflection and action are necessary to overcome many of the cultural barriers to integration that exist. We then provide strategies for this integration that need to be addressed at the institutional level. The individual strategies we recommend can be sustained for a limited time if institutional support is not provided. Combined action on the individual and institutional levels can result in greater integration of each element of learning, ultimately enhancing students' overall experiences and outcomes.

HISTORY AND CURRENT CONDITIONS

I was enormously struck by the fact that there are two cultures in the academy today. There's the culture of the classroom and there's the culture of life outside the classroom, and these are enormously divided. The classroom culture has a clear academic goal and on many campuses the out-of-classroom experience has no guidance, little purpose, and often the climate can be described as low-grade decadence. (Boyer Address 1988, p. 4)

When exploring the disintegration of social, emotional, and intellectual development in higher education one can begin with the debate concerning the question of the appropriate purpose and nature of the curriculum in American higher education. Has it been the purpose of the curriculum to prepare individuals for lives of professional practice in such fields as the clergy, medicine, law, and education? Or has the purpose of higher education been to produce well-rounded men and women who have undertaken a rigorous course of study across all manner of disciplines, receiving a liberal arts education in the best sense of the word? Has the curriculum consisted of only that which takes place in the classroom, or has it been the nature of the curriculum to take into account the whole of a student's experience—that which happens between and around classes as well as in class? These options represent both ends of a continuum—one that has swung from pole to pole at various times in the history of higher education, and one that has been influenced by a number of factors.

The purposes of this section are to describe how American higher education, especially during the last century and a half, evolved to the point at which the intellectual, social, and emotional development of college students has disintegrated to the extent cited above; to identify the current barriers to integrating the intellectual, social, and emotional divide; and to bring to light the conditions and elements that are serving as potential facilitators to integrating these elements.

We see two distinct, though related, divisions that have developed in higher education: the splitting of emotional elements from the intellectual development, and division of the social from the cognitive elements of learning. In the evolution of this separation, it is possible to trace the effects of a number of forces at work: the role of positivism in defining ways of knowing; the increasing specialization and fragmentation of the academic disciplines; the fragmentation of the faculty role into three spheres of research, teaching, and service (as well as the predominant emphasis on research); the resultant emphasis of student affairs professionals on students' noncognitive development; and the fragmentation of the student experience on campus and the subsequent loss of a unified college community. We argue that these changes contributed to a breakdown in the social community on campus and encouraged the further fragmentation of student learning by dividing social processes away from the learning process.

Historical Development of the Separation of Social and Emotional Processes From Student Learning

One of the first elements of learning to be shaved away in Western education was any area dealing with internal and unobservable states, such as emotions, aesthetics, values, and motivations. If something could not be observed, it could not be measured; therefore, it was not real and could not be considered a basis for knowledge and truth. This concept was grounded in the positivist paradigm—the belief that "nothing is knowable except as it is susceptible to empirical demonstration, that only that which is confirmable in public sensory experience qualifies as genuine knowledge, and therefore, that values (as distinct from facts) must be consigned to the domain of feelings, tastes, and purely subjective preferences" (Lucas 1985, p. 166). This was grounded in the philosophy of, among others, Rene Descartes, whose writings espoused the split between mind and body, between internal mentation and objective reality (Lucas 1985). This pervasive belief system subordinated nonintellectual activities to rational, empirically based knowledge (Caple 1996; Kuh, Shedd, and Whitt 1987).

The role of positivism in placing emphasis on intellectual development continues to be a major barrier to other modes of thinking about intellectual, emotional, and social development. It is not difficult to see a connection between the positivist paradigm and higher education's emphasis on cognitive development. If a belief in the mind/body split is the norm (so much so that it is not even questioned, and positivism holds sway over other ways of knowing, then a narrowly defined intellectual development is no surprise. Specialization is the path to the continued creation of knowledge, which also is a prime goal of higher education, especially in American universities today. Although emotional and moral development is acknowledged, it is not associated with nor is it given the weight or attention that is devoted to intellectual development. "It is not surprising, given the pervasive influence of this positivist belief system, that students' intellectual and personal development are thought to be discrete, mutually exclusive domains and student affairs work is viewed as ancillary to the primary mission of the academy" (Kuh, Shedd, and Whitt 1987, p. 256). The emphasis on individualism and competition, as opposed to social elements of collaboration and community, has its roots in these tenets of higher education—that our way of knowing is characterized by objectivity, analysis, experimentation, and the separation of subject and object (Brown 1990; Palmer 1987). And, although alternative paradigms have been proposed and are being explored, the full impact of this shift has yet to be seen or understood (Lucas 1985).

Given the wholeheartedness with which positivist reasoning was embraced—initially in the natural sciences and eventually in social sciences as well—it is no surprise that the German university model and its emphasis on research and scholarship so strongly influenced American higher education. Separating fact from feelings also contributed to the gulf between those seen as responsible for students' intellectual growth and those seen as responsible for students' social and emotional growth. If, as discussed below, the growth in the size of institutions and in the population of student affairs professionals allowed the social processes of college to be removed from the classroom, the acceptance of the positivist paradigm as the only way of knowing in higher education forced emotional influences out of the classroom as well.

The separation of social from intellectual processes in learning can be seen in the evolution of higher education in this country. The most influential factor in this regard was the shift from a liberal arts model of education to the emergence of the German university model and its emphasis on research and scholarship. Although much more can be said about this aspect of change in American higher education (and has been said, most notably by Brubacher and Rudy

Although emotional and moral development is acknowledged, it is not associated with nor is it given the weight or attention that is devoted to intellectual development.

[1976], but also by Chickering and Reisser [1993] and Fenske [1989]), we will only note that the rise of the German university model allowed—indeed, compelled—faculty members to specialize in their particular discipline, which in turn drove the emergence of the elective system in the curriculum which encouraged students to specialize and be narrowly focused in their studies.

The rise of the university model, the increased specialization within disciplines, the increased focus on faculty research as a preeminent form of scholarship, and the creation of the elective system in the curriculum all influenced, and were influenced by, changes in the role of faculty and the role of students. In this section we review some of the relevant literature that addresses this history.

We begin at the turn of the 20th century, when the separation of intellectual development from social and emotional processes began to be noticed, and noted. It was at that time that President Eliot of Harvard College was instrumental in the rise of the elective system on that campus and influential at other campuses as well.* From 1869-1909, during his tenure as president, Eliot oversaw the dismantling of a rigid set of course requirements which were uniform for all undergraduates and the rise of a "laissez faire" system of elective courses with few restrictions or requirements (Jencks and Riesman 1962). As students gained the freedom to choose their courses and faculty gained the freedom to teach increasingly specialized courses, "the 19th-century hostility between faculty and student was abated by the increasing indifference of both to education" (p. 734).

Instead, faculty became more involved with their specialized avenues of research, and students "continued to escape, not only into their clubs, but into an increasingly professional round of extracurricular activities where exigent standards of performance—whether in writing, dramatics, or athletics—attracted rather than repelled recruits" (Jencks and Riesman 1962, p. 738). Faculty took less notice of what happened beyond their classrooms, and students used their freedom to pursue interests beyond their academics. The continuity that had resulted from small numbers of people intensively study-

*Although our initial attention to Harvard may seem unrepresentative of what was happening at other institutions, at the time Harvard was in many ways a bellwether of future reforms. Reforms and movements that began at Harvard spread throughout the country in similar forms.

ing the same topics, as had been the norm since the development of the colonial colleges, was interrupted.

Such was the state of college curricula in the early 1900s. The student experience had become one of fragmentation, a separation of academic endeavors from extracurricular activities. And extracurricular activities were a force with which to be reckoned. In *Campus Life: Undergraduate Cultures From the End of the Eighteenth Century to the Present*, Horowitz chronicled the oscillations between what she called "college life" (the extracurriculum) and the attention paid to a student's program of study (1987). She described "college men" as those who formed the majority of the student body and were more intent on college life—athletics, social clubs, fraternities, newspapers, and other student organizations—than they were on their courses. "Outsiders" tended to be those students who were intent on their studies, called "grinds" by college men. Horowitz also pointed out that at any period in time one could find a variety of these types of students on a single campus, although the proportions might change or a certain type might gain in popularity and visibility. She cited the efforts of many college presidents and faculty members to discourage the proliferation of college life and refocus student energies within the classroom, but acknowledged:

> By the 1920s the administrators of most colleges and universities had come to an accommodation with college life. Not only was it assumed to be normal; its long-term benefits were now clear. Alumni with fond memories of college days emerged to endow alma mater. Football games cultivated undergraduate loyalty, especially when the school had winning teams. Moreover, the codes of college life—however hostile to the academic enterprise—served to govern student behavior. As colleges and universities grew to a large size, their administrators perceived the value of communal order, even one patrolled by students. The trick was to harness college life, to limit its hedonism and more destructive elements, and to emphasize its relation to citizenship and service (1987, p. 108).

Horowitz's description of college life reflects the little thought given at the time to the possibility of social, emotional, and intellectual development being fostered outside the classroom. The focus at many institutions was on social and peer control of student behavior.

Some institutions, while acknowledging the important influence of the peer culture, tried to shape it toward intellectual ends. Chief among those who tried was Abbott Lawrence Lowell, president of Harvard (1909-1933). His influence culminated in 1930 with the opening of the Harvard House System (Jencks and Riesman 1962) through which he hoped to integrate intellectual work with social cohesion. The houses consisted of the usual bedrooms and bathrooms of conventional dormitories, but each was "enriched" by the addition of a library and lounge space for studying; the presence of a House master (a senior faculty member), senior tutors (junior faculty members), and tutors (graduate students) who held tutorial sessions in the house for residents; and a dining hall in which students and faculty met daily on an informal basis. Because of their relative luxury and the opportunities provided to students to converse with faculty, Jencks and Riesman speculated that the houses were meant to "seduce" students into becoming interested in intellectual topics and were an academic alternative to social clubs or sports teams.

The purpose of the Harvard House System foreshadows the programs that use social and emotional processes to enhance intellectual development under way today which are discussed later in the report. By taking advantage of social dynamics—friendships formed through shared, everyday experiences such as dining and discussing topics of mutual interest—Harvard hoped to encourage intellectual development. The separation of the academic content from the rest of the college experience, which had been exacerbated by the elective system, was to be linked back together by efforts outside of the classroom.

The tensions felt at Harvard between students' social and academic lives were felt elsewhere and were addressed in fashions similar to the House system. Bennington College, founded in 1932, stressed the interrelated community formed by its students and faculty. Newcomb studied the attitudes of students at Bennington between 1935 and 1939 and described the informal nature of classes which were "conducted as workshops, studios, laboratories, or as discussion groups far more frequently than by the lecture method" (1943, p. 7). Not only were class arrangements different from other colleges, there were "no 'extracurricular' clubs or organizations . . . the educational assumption being that if it [was] worthwhile for a student to carry on a given sort of activity, it should [have been] fully legitimized within her program of college work" (p. 6). Such a degree of integration between academic and social endeavors no doubt was facilitated by the small size of the institution (250 students, 50 faculty), yet the fact that it was founded upon such principles suggests that the Bennington faculty and students did not want to continue to separate those endeavors.

Reform efforts were happening at large campuses as well. The curricular reform efforts of Alexander Meiklejohn at the University of Wisconsin provided another model of an integrated core of courses. In place from 1927-1932 at the University of Wisconsin, Meiklejohn's Experimental College curriculum contrasted with the earlier popularity of the elective system, as it emphasized the holistic nature of information across courses. Furthermore, the curriculum "required students to develop a personal point of view, to connect the ideas in the classroom with the 'real world'" (Gabelnick et al. 1990, p. 11). Meiklejohn's model inspired other types of core curricula, such as the "Experiment at Berkeley" from 1965-1969, and the use of the "Great Books," at St. John's College in Maryland and New Mexico (Brubacher and Rudy 1976).

While reforms were being instituted in isolated areas, forces continued to separate the work of students and faculty members and maintain the fragmentation among emotional, social, and intellectual elements of learning. Student culture was connecting social and emotional processes but in ways that did not necessarily contribute to holistic learning as we have described it. For example, Newcomb studied interactions within student peer groups (1962). He argued that the educational objectives of higher education were not being furthered by peer groups in most American colleges because the objectives of the peer groups were different from those of the institution. Furthermore, the peer groups that formed naturally among students were not the same ones that formed within classes. Especially in larger institutions, students from the same classes seldom met outside of classes and so the opportunities to continue intellectual conversations begun in class were lost. This again was portrayed more recently through Moffatt's study at Rutgers University (1989).

Perhaps because reforms designed to integrate students' experiences and learning had been implemented sporadically and in isolated circumstances and were based upon the concerted efforts of a few individuals, they were unable to overcome the many barriers they faced. Competing demands on faculty time and a student culture that was driven by issues other than intellectual development contributed to the disintegration of a sense of holistic learning.

It is no coincidence that the field of student affairs in higher education was emerging at the same time Harvard and other institutions were seeking ways to connect student and academic life. As more faculty members were trained in the German tradition of research and scholarship, the emphasis on their role in the development of the whole student diminished. Colleges created the new positions of

dean of men and dean of women, which were filled by faculty members whose responsibility was to "supervise the non-academic life of students and to advise and inspire them" (Horowitz 1987, p. 111). Student conduct and their spiritual and moral development were delegated to these deans of men and deans of women (Williamson 1961). Services that faculty traditionally had performed, such as personal counseling, academic advising, vocational guidance, student discipline, admissions, and registering students for courses, were needed by growing numbers of students and were delegated to an emerging set of personnel professionals (Appleton, Briggs, and Rhatigan 1978; Mueller 1961; Williamson 1961).

The adaptation of the German model of higher education established research and scholarly activities as priorities at many institutions; encouraged faculty to emphasize research and specialization; and diminished the importance of personal growth, general studies, and ethical dimensions of higher education (Kuh, Shedd, and Whitt 1987). This could not have happened to the degree that it did if it were not for the emergence of student affairs professionals who picked up what no longer was a priority for faculty. "Because student affairs workers performed tasks that many faculty members no longer considered integral to the academic enterprise, the faculty understandably came to regard student affairs functions as separate from the academic core of the institution" (Kuh, Shedd, and Whitt 1987, p. 253).

Other forces contributed to the fragmentation of the college community and the further dichotomization of intellectual and social development. The 1960s saw dramatic increases in the number of public colleges and universities, which caused an increase in students of more diverse backgrounds, interests, and needs for higher education (Appleton, Briggs, and Rhatigan 1978). Not only did the numbers of students grow, but their increasing diversity made college communities that had been built on the commonality of students' backgrounds and experiences a thing of the past. At many institutions the roles of faculty and student affairs professionals spread further apart, as the "growth in numbers of students, complexity of organization, and heterogeneity in purposes and problems forced colleges to designate special officers and agencies to meet the problems that traditional officers could not handle" (Shaffer 1993, p. 163). The booming increases that colleges and universities were to see in the coming decades would further contribute to the demise of the college community that Boyer (1988; 1990) and others later would lament.

It is not difficult to imagine how this confluence of forces—specialization of the disciplines, emphasis on research and scholarship, emergence of student affairs professionals, and the pervasive positivist paradigm—led to the point at which the intellectual development of students was seen not only as the primary purpose of higher education but as completely distinct from social and emotional processes. To be sure, institutions of higher education took seriously the responsibility of acting *in loco parentis* for their students, and student affairs professionals were receiving advanced training in growing numbers. However, higher education had reached the point at which two forces influenced students. The larger of the two concerned the interaction of students and faculty and the resulting intellectual development. The smaller of the two concerned the interaction of students and their peers; students and student affairs professionals; and the social, emotional, and physical well-being of the students.

Current Cultural Barriers to Integrating Social, Emotional, and Intellectual Development

The aforementioned historical developments form one part of a cultural barrier to integrating social, emotional, and intellectual processes of student learning, in part because history represents an important part of higher education's culture. In this section we focus on the current aspects of higher education's culture that reinforce the disintegration of emotional, social, and intellectual development. This discussion includes a description of salient aspects of the culture of higher education, including faculty norms and rewards, student affairs norms, student culture, and a notion of what constitutes a college community. Our point in presenting and discussing barriers to bridging the emotional/social/intellectual divides is to bring to conscious level some of the factors that make this divide so insidious. Having made these barriers conscious, we turn our attention in subsequent sections to overcoming them.

Higher-education culture

The forces that shaped the roles of faculty and student affairs professionals during the early part of the 20th century remain largely unchanged despite exhortations during the last few years for faculty to teach more and for student affairs professionals to try harder to cooperate with faculty members. If anything, the lines between the two sides are more firmly drawn:

> An invidious hierarchy of professionals prevails on most campuses. The 'pecking order' in place reflects common notions that intellectual development is the higher and proper ground for faculty, and that psychosocial development is the lower and proper ground for student life staff. . . . The prevailing hierarchy is rooted in an impoverished conception of the teaching-learning process, one that improperly dichotomizes development in the affective and cognitive domains. Although some aspects of human development other than cognitive are addressed in formal courses, most are left to chance or to the student-lifers. And some, such as artistic-aesthetic sensibility, are left largely undernourished (Stringer, Steckler, and Johnson 1988, p. 46).

The term "higher-education culture" is misleading because the assertion that there is a single culture is questionable (Kuh and Whitt 1988). To understand all sides of the issue, it may be more helpful to recognize three broad cultures within institutions of higher education—those of the faculty, student affairs professionals, and students—although within each of these many subcultures exist. Not only are these three cultures broad, but they each have their respective broad literature bases. For thorough discussions of these areas, we refer the reader to Horowitz (1987, student culture); Kuh (1993a, student affairs culture); Kuh and Whitt (1988, higher-education culture); Tierney (1990, faculty culture); and Tierney and Rhoads (1994, faculty culture). Multiple subcultures notwithstanding, by examining the three main cultures many barriers become evident. Faculty and student affairs cultures are discussed together and followed by a separate discussion of student culture.

Much of the lack of change in faculty and student affairs roles can be attributed to strong cultural norms throughout higher education that reinforce these roles. Brown refers to these as differences in orientation and writes:

> Barriers arise from both real and perceived differences between academicians and student affairs professionals. There are differences in the organizational structures and reward systems, in background and training, in norms and cultures, and in goals and priorities. . . . Traditionally, faculty have considered the primary functions of the university to be creating, preserving, and transmitting knowledge while promoting and safeguarding the so-called life of the mind. Their professional rewards have followed from these values. Moreover, recognition, promotion, and tenure at most institutions are based more on scholarly contribution to an academic discipline than on professional contributions to the education of students or the welfare of the institution (1990, pp. 246-47).

Love, Kuh, MacKay, and Hardy point to further distinction in the basic values of faculty and student affairs (1993). They point out that while faculty are focused on higher order needs (cognitive development, for example), student affairs professionals are focused both on basic (such as orientation to college and providing residence and dining services) and higher order (leadership development, multicultural awareness and diversity programming, and counseling) needs. Love et al. argue that most faculty perceive student affairs professionals (if they perceive them at all) as providing for basic needs only (1993). Other differences in cultural expectations include the observation that faculty value autonomy over collaboration; whereas, given organizational structures and tasks, student affairs professionals value collaboration over autonomy. Faculty value thinking and reflecting over doing; student affairs professionals tend to value doing over thinking and reflecting.

In the section about facilitating conditions, it is noted that efforts are under way to change the priorities facing faculty placed on research, teaching, and service such as redefining what constitutes scholarship (Boyer 1990) and creating administrative positions to focus on undergraduate students and their education ('Student Focus' Stressed at Muhlenberg 1994). These types of efforts, however, need extended—and sometimes extensive—support to take hold, and even then they take a long time to influence the faculty and student affairs subcultures as well as the larger overall culture.

Another barrier facing faculty and student affairs professionals in the development of holistic approaches to students' social and intellectual development is their training and socialization.

> *Faculty are provided little if any background about the nature and structure of the organizations in which they are likely to spend their careers. In addition, faculty receive little training in performing the task to which they will devote much of their professional time—teaching. Until recently at least, few faculty had any conception of how students learn or of the impact of the outside-the-classroom environment on student performance and retention* (Brown 1990, p. 246).

Historically, this has been as true for full-time faculty members as it has been for teaching assistants. Student affairs professionals, though exposed to developmental theory in most master's preparation programs, are socialized into a profession in which cognition and the intellect is deemphasized, as evidenced through their professional journals (Kuh et al. 1986).

As indicated previously, student affairs culture holds as an espoused, though not completely enacted, value of holistic student development. Related to the emphasis on social and emotional development is the dominant student affairs cultural view holding that intellectual development is restricted to the classroom or classroomlike venues, while social and emotional development is restricted to out-of-class experiences. This is a limited view of student learning and development. Fortunately, recent research and literature (seen, for example, in Baxter Magolda 1992, 1995; Kuh, Schuh, and Whitt 1991; Terenzini et al. 1992, *The Student Learning Imperative*) have been influencing the discourse in the field and may be providing the impetus that will assist with the more full enactment of holistic student development. On the academic side, it can be noted that many of the humanities and social-science disciplines deal with broad matters of life including feelings, relationships, and moral and ethical decisions and their consequences. Whether these aspects of the disciplines are enacted upon in the classroom, the possibility to bring social and emotional issues into the classroom exists.

The values and cultural norms of faculty and student affairs professionals contribute to an inability on the part of institutions to change quickly in response to changing needs of students or demands from groups external to the institution. The pervasiveness of these cultural values is what makes their influence so strong and so resistant to change.

Finally, the culture of higher education includes the assumption that while moral and ethical development occur while students are in college, they are not the purview of educators (that is, faculty) and thus have been relegated to student affairs personnel. This is an extension of the historical development of college curricula presented earlier in this section. The lingering effects of the 1960s—when students pushed college professors and administrators further out of their personal lives—and our reluctance in the 1980s to challenge the beliefs of others for fear of treading on their rights as individuals combined to create a climate on campuses that sidestepped the examination of values.

The works of Perry (1970), Kohlberg (1971), and Gilligan (1982) all are seen as related to cognitive development and are discussed as such, but the related development of values and morals are viewed as off-limits by many college educators. It is safer for faculty to leave topics such as morals and values in the hands of those seen as outside the educational mission of the institution (student affairs professionals and campus ministry, for example) and remain focused on the value-free content of the disciplines.

The values and cultural norms of faculty and student affairs professionals contribute to an inability on the part of institutions to change quickly in response to changing needs of students . . .

Student culture. Generally, student life has cleaved off from academics. Newcomb and Wilson noted that the spheres of the peer group and those of the intellect overlap only slightly (1966). Astin also noted that the student culture of traditional-aged students has become dominated by desires for self-fulfillment, self-enhancement, and financial security (1993). These students are encouraged to view their lives in fragmentary ways; what they do in the classroom is disconnected from their lives outside the classroom, and what they do at work is disconnected from who they are and what they do at home.

An ethnographic study of college students carried out from 1959 to 1961 looked at the importance of grades in the lives of the students (Becker, Geer, and Hughes 1968). The study concluded that students at a large public Midwestern university placed a great deal of emphasis on grades—what grades they had received and what they thought they might receive. On the surface this appeared to be a concern with intellectual development; however, it actually was due to the fact that grades were used to determine in which dorm students lived or to which fraternity or sorority they could belong. Place of residence and Greek affiliation were the key signs of prestige on that campus, so students paid significant attention to grades and what minimum grade point average they needed to get into a desirable residence. Instead of being a study about students and their intellectual development, it is more about how students positioned themselves in desirable social strata. As shown in other studies, the social concerns of students were driving their academic efforts (see, for example, Goodsell 1993; Lamont 1979; Leemon 1972; Moffatt 1989). What took place in the classroom and the attention paid to classwork outside of the classroom were heavily influenced by nonacademic issues, and a culture of anti-intellectualism pervaded many campuses (Horowitz 1987).

Conceptions of college community
If some degree of common values, common experience, and communication constitute the foundation of community, and some sense of community is necessary for institutional transformation, then higher education faces a monumental barrier. Brown effectively summarizes the barriers to bridging students' social and intellectual development, drawing

together the elements of culture, changing student demographics, and strained or nonexistent relationships between
student affairs professionals and faculty (1990):

> *Although the term* academic community *is still a part of
> the higher-education lexicon, the reality at all but the
> smallest schools is lack of communication and lack of
> shared experience among the many subcultures that
> constitute an institution of higher education. The size
> of contemporary colleges and universities, their frag-
> mented organizational structures and confusion over
> goals, and the adversarial relationships between faculty
> and administration on all too many campuses con-
> tribute to the problem. In addition, the demands on
> students' time (with many working half time or more to
> help pay the cost of higher education today), the
> increasing proportions of commuting and adult stu-
> dents, the competitiveness promoted by college policies
> and practices, and the very diversity that we claim to
> value are all barriers to creating and sustaining a
> sense of community* (Brown 1990, p. 262).

Calls for a return to a more unified campus or academic
community have been frequent (Boyer 1990; Palmer 1990;
Study Group 1984), yet the possibility of a common notion
of community is as questionable as it is for notions of a
single higher-education culture.

Tinto (1993) writes that it is important to nurture many
student subcultures within a single institution because all
students are not alike and do not have the same needs. By
nurturing and sustaining many subcultures, institutions can
increase the chances that students will feel as if they fit in
somewhere. Perhaps, then, the notion that there should be
(or even could be) a single, unified campus community is as
much a barrier to bridging students' social, emotional, and
intellectual development as is the actual absence of such a
community. Tierney (1993) speaks of communities of difference—communities in which different values and different
experiences are valued and nurtured. Shifts in student
demographics (such as increases in students of color, older
students, and part-time students) demand that our notions of
campus community be reexamined. For faculty members to
yearn for the days when students were better-prepared and

had more leisure time to seek out faculty in their offices or for student affairs professionals to wish that all students still had no family obligations and could attend evening programs is to miss the current intellectual and professional challenges. It also is to miss the excitement that results from meeting such challenges.

This brief discussion of barriers serves to highlight the difficulties involved in integrating the emotional, social, and intellectual processes of student learning. Although the pendulum of curricular integration has swung back and forth throughout the history of higher education in this country, the pervasive, competing cultures that have developed have maintained the momentum of the current swing away from integration. An understanding of these barriers to integration allows us to turn our attention more successfully toward conditions that facilitate integration.

Facilitating Conditions

Facilitating conditions are those circumstances, issues, and changes that are helping to create conditions in which intellectual, social, and emotional processes more easily might be integrated in students' learning experiences. These conditions are helping to create climates and cultural enclaves in which changes are taking place. They are the necessary but insufficient conditions to accomplish the task of integration. It is due, in part, to the present confluence of facilitating conditions that this report is written at this particular time. The facilitating conditions we describe are a continuing paradigm shift in social sciences and education, the emergence of disciplines that incorporate the impact of social processes and issues of affect, current reform efforts, and external pressure on colleges and universities, especially in the area of outcomes assessment.

Paradigm shift

The positivist paradigm that is consistent with predominant modes of thought in many fields increasingly has come under attack (Lincoln and Guba 1989). Lucas, in writing about paradigm shifts in the natural and social sciences, traced changes in predominant theories in physics and psychology (1985). He noted the changes from early "rigid reductionism and positivism," where science "[dealt] only with hard, objective facts," to recent patterns of holistic thought (p. 166). Citing the dominance of Cartesian influence on natural science, Lucas delineated the paradigm shifts in various areas. In physics, thought moved first from particle theory, then to wave theory, and then to a combination of the two.

In psychology, the early emphasis was on becoming a natural (and therefore legitimate) science, so the focus was on behavior as the only objective, observable part of the field. Early developmental psychologists also began to focus almost exclusively on skills and tasks associated with the natural sciences and mathematics and de-emphasized development-related intuition, emotion, spatial perception, and music (Kurfiss 1983).

In the 1960s, the attention of educational and psychological researchers turned to such topics as the interpersonal relationships between teachers and students (Katz 1962; Tiberius and Billson 1991) and the formation of peer groups and their influence on students' identity formation (Newcomb 1962). Katz used the psychological term *transference* to describe the interactions between students and faculty, acknowledging that such interactions could be major, if misunderstood, factors in learning. Personal interaction introduced "a bothersome element into the supposedly dispassionate intercourse of minds. Yet it is a potent vehicle for learning, mislearning, and not learning" (Katz 1962, p. 386).

Part of this paradigm shift includes the widespread acceptance of alternative research methodologies, especially qualitative research. The past decade has seen a significant increase in the number of qualitative studies focusing on student experience (for example, Baxter Magolda 1992; Belenky et al. 1986; Kuh et al. 1991; Moffatt 1989), and especially the experiences of those students who have been at the margins of American higher education, such as students of color (Attinasi 1989; Murguia, Padilla, and Pavel 1991). One outcome that has emerged from these studies is the significant influence of social and emotional influences on students' ability to learn and succeed in higher education.

Although positivist methodologies still carry tremendous weight, naturalistic, qualitative methods are gaining ground. Through their use of inductive analysis, the attention paid to matters of context and grounded theory-building facilitates a focus on the integration of social and emotional processes with intellectual development (Glaser and Strauss 1967; Strauss and Corbin 1990). However, despite changes in other sciences, in educational-research methodology, and in education processes, the influence of positivism still pervades. Palmer indicates that the "modern physicist may have abandoned the image of atoms floating in the void, but [higher education still has] a culture of individualism which mirrors that discredited worldview" (1983, p. xiv). So, although a paradigm shift can be identified, its effects only recently are being felt.

The emergence of new disciplines

New disciplines have emerged continually throughout the history of American higher education. In fact, this tendency has contributed to the continual fragmentation of the faculty community. Newly emerging disciplines such as women's studies; Pan-African studies; and gay, lesbian, and bisexual studies are somewhat different in that they have turned their focus of research back on the process and organization of education and are critiquing the traditional role and culture of academia. They appear to be part of the larger paradigm shift occurring in education. Additionally, the study of higher education and student affairs has contributed significantly to the research base that underlies this report.

In addition to new disciplines, new and broader definitions of scholarship are emerging (Boyer 1990; Rice and Sheridan 1989). These definitions recognize that effective integration, application, and communication of knowledge, as well as the discovery or creation of knowledge through research, are viable forms of scholarly activity (Boyer 1990). An example of this is the set of classroom assessment techniques that Cross and Angelo called upon college faculty to practice (1992). They encouraged faculty members to experiment with and test hypotheses about their instructional methods and their effects on student learning. In this way one's own teaching becomes an object of scholarship.

Current reform efforts

Like the institutions attempting reform at other points in this century, some institutions today appear to be reversing direction and moving back toward the consistency and coherence thought to be provided by core requirements or by a general-education core. Calls for reform during the last decade have recommended that colleges and universities refocus their efforts to be consistent with their mission statements, provide more coherence to their curricula, and create "community" by structuring similar experiences for all students (Boyer 1987; *Campus Life* 1990; Study Group 1984). As Brown suggests:

> *The lists of objectives or outcomes that have emerged from the many efforts to overhaul general education bear remarkable resemblances. Competence in reasoning and critical thinking, effective communication skills, tolerance for ambiguity, understanding different cultures, esthetic appreciation, ability to make value-based distinctions and decisions, and understanding social institutions and of the relationships between the individual and society are some of the commonalities among the goals that have been identified* (1990, p. 254).

Related to the current reform movement is the ongoing presence of the Continuous Quality Improvement movement and its merging with the assessment movement, especially through the efforts of the American Association for Higher Education. It remains to be seen what lasting impact this will have on higher education, but it specifically recognizes the importance of cultural change in institutions of higher education. That alone makes it quite different from past reform movements.

External pressures
External pressures have been brought to bear on higher education as well, as parents, employers, and legislatures question the cost and outcomes of higher education. The assessment movement can be seen as a direct result of the hesitancy of these constituencies to endorse the status quo. Although a potential barrier to integration, changes in student demographics also may contain elements that serve to facilitate the integration of intellectual, social, and emotional processes in the learning process. "Research has documented the differences in learning styles, academic values, and personal characteristics between the so-called new students and the more affluent and academically oriented college students of the fifties and sixties" (Cross 1976; Davis and

Schroeder 1983) (Brown 1990, p. 251). Other external pressures that are demanding the attention of those in higher education include the shrinking global community, increasingly pervasive technology, and financial strain.

As indicated earlier in this section, the presence of facilitating conditions does not ensure that necessary changes will be made. Instead, these conditions create a context in which change becomes more possible. Leadership, hard work, and additional strategies are needed if future students will experience an educational experience in which intellectual, social, and emotional elements are integrated. The general public is demanding that education be more efficient and relevant and do a better job of preparing our citizens for participation in the workforce and society of the future. As institutions scramble to find methods that work, it remains to be seen whether our practice will emphasize the necessity of the reciprocal, mutually shaping intellectual, social, and emotional elements of student learning. The following sections describe research that substantiates the interrelationship of emotional, social, and intellectual aspects of learning and individual and institutional strategies to overcome some of the aforementioned barriers and promote integration.

THE LINKS AMONG INTELLECTUAL, SOCIAL, AND EMOTIONAL ELEMENTS OF LEARNING: THE RESEARCH

We have examined the historical and cultural context that has developed in American higher education related to the fragmenting of the disciplines, the college community, and, ultimately, the learning process. That development has resulted in significant barriers and challenges facing faculty, student affairs professionals, and administrators who attempt to facilitate the holistic education of college students, especially at four-year research institutions. In this section we return to the axiom that a student's intellectual development is influenced by social and emotional factors.

Recall our argument from the first section—that the mutually influential nature of cognitive, social, and affective development is accepted as fact, but that many of our individual actions and organizational behaviors indicate otherwise. To reinforce the need to understand the powerful influences connecting intellectual, social, and affective development, we further expand upon our conceptual framework and describe some of the research that supports it.

Knowing and being actively aware that cognitive, social, and affective development are interrelated is one step toward grounding this axiom in practice. Another important issue is how and in what conditions they are mutually influential. In this section, research is presented that substantiates the links between the various diads of intellectual, social, and emotional processes as well as the interconnectedness among all three. In a sense, because the evidence indicates that these processes are linked, the links that have to be made among intellectual, social, and emotional elements of learning must be made in the minds of higher-education educators.

The influences of social processes and emotional elements on learning may be—and most often are—ignored, but that does not mean they are not influencing the learning process. By ignoring these influences educators allow this instructive void to be filled in ways that may be detrimental to the learning process. Peers exert a great deal of influence on how the academic enterprise is interpreted by students. This widespread student culture influences the motivations, attitudes, values, and beliefs about learning that students carry with them into the classroom. Faculty may ignore the emotional states of their students, but negative feelings such as depression, thoughts of suicide, and horrors of abuse and neglect; fears related to parental divorce, finances, or social acceptance; and positive feelings such as hope, curiosity, love, optimism, excitement about a relationship, or pride in an accomplishment all are carried into the classroom and exist as students struggle to understand their work and apply it to their lives. Higher education professionals must recognize their students as complete individuals—as thinking, feeling, social beings—as a first step toward creating a holistic learning process.

Cognitive and Social Processes

Most learning and development take place in a social context. The stimulation that causes such precursors to learning as cognitive dissonance (Festinger 1957) or disequilibrium (Piaget 1928) often is an external stimulation and most often comes from other people in the environment. Yet, the history and tradition of American higher education celebrate and revere the lone scholar and researcher. Individualism, independence, autonomy, and competition are values inherent in higher education's academic culture (Love et al. 1993). Extending this cultural influence to developmental theory, Piaget's recognition of the role of social forces in children's development often is overlooked (1926). Elsewhere, the role of supportive (and challenging) others, groups, or teams in the process of knowledge development has been de-emphasized or ignored. Competition is traditionally championed over cooperation, although much research shows cooperation to be superior to competition in terms of achievement and feelings of well-being (Kohn 1986).

Only recently has the role of interpersonal interaction, communication, and support been discussed with regard to how the ideas and knowledge of what is perceived as an individual project developed. For example, Perry's Scheme, as Perry himself argued, is the product of the work and thoughts of at least 30 people (1981). Recognizing the influence of others also might be beneficial for the cognitive development of college students. The social aspects of cognitive development, though recognized and accepted as fact, often are not attended to or given credit.

Perhaps the strongest statements in the literature related to social, affective, and cognitive development have been made about the connection between social processes and cognitive development (for example, Baxter Magolda 1992, 1995; Chickering and Reisser 1993; King and Baxter Magolda

1996). Chickering and Reisser point out that relationships provide powerful learning experiences and opportunities to enhance cognitive development (1993). These relationships include out-of-class faculty-student interaction, which consistently has been shown to be very influential in student growth and outcomes (Astin 1993; Pascarella and Terenzini 1991); pedagogical interactions between faculty and students (Brophy 1985; Good 1987); social and academic interaction among students (Bean and Creswell 1980; Harnett 1965; Kuh 1995; Weinstein 1989); students' perceptions of an instructor's social and academic behaviors (Weinstein 1989); and the effects of cultural and other social differences on social interaction within the classroom (Li 1992; Flores, Cousin, and Diaz 1991).

... current scholars and researchers have found it difficult to separate cognitive skills from social processes.

Generally, current scholars and researchers have found it difficult to separate cognitive skills from social processes. In fact, the entire area of research now known as social cognition is premised on the belief that learning occurs in a social context and that one's ability to interact effectively with others requires some level of cognitive ability (and vice versa). "A cognitively complex individual is better able to adapt to the demands of changing social situations than is a less complex individual. . . . Cognitively complex persons are more skilled at taking the others' perspective and, therefore, should be more effective in sending and receiving messages" (Rubin and Henzl 1984, p. 264).

Many recent theories of cognitive development in college students more clearly recognize the role of social elements (Baxter Magolda 1992, 1995; Belenky et al. 1986; Gilligan 1982). For example, Baxter Magolda (1992, 1995) incorporates social relationships into her scheme of cognitive development and, in fact, indicated that one of the principles guiding her work in exploring students' intellectual development was that "ways of knowing and patterns within them are socially constructed" (1992, p. 20). She refers to this as relational knowing characterized by attachment and connection. This connection is with others and with what is known.

"One of the most powerful messages in the students' stories was that the ability to develop a distinctive voice stems from defining learning as constructing meaning jointly with others" (Baxter Magolda 1992, p. xiv). Baxter Magolda contrasts relational knowing with patterns of impersonal knowing, which are those highlighted by separation and abstraction. Impersonal knowing also is characterized by autonomy, objectivity, and rationality, all of which are recognized and celebrated by the positivist paradigm that is dominant in higher education (Baxter Magolda 1995). Baxter Magolda argues for a place for both in the learning process, though the concern is that the current culture emphasizes the latter.

Josselson, in her work on women's identity development, identified the role of supportive people in moving beyond foreclosure—a state of premature resolution of one's identity (1987). Belenky et al. indicated that a willingness to ask questions and add to discussion enhances intellectual development (1986). Their stage of connected knowing reflects the importance of social relationships and interaction in the process of cognitive development. It also emphasizes the importance of connecting theory and learning to personal experiences. Baxter Magolda (1992) and Belenky et al. (1986), focusing on issues of gender and cognitive development, indicated that women value connectedness or social relationships in their learning experiences to a greater extent than do men, but that both men and women benefit from connectedness and positive social relationship in the learning process. This gender-related pattern also is consistent with the findings of Springer et al., who found that "time spent socializing with friends was more positively related to gains in orientations toward learning for self-understanding for women than for men" (1995, p. 16).

Lundeberg and Diemert Moch (1995) discovered that an emphasis on connected knowing through collaborative supplemental instruction (peer-led discussion groups) helped increase the number of female nursing students who successfully completed required science courses—courses that were archetypal examples of separate knowing (Belenky et al. 1986). The culture that developed in these peer groups was characterized by a spirit of cooperation, community, a shift in power from leaders to students, and increased risk-taking. Lundeberg and Diemert Moch identified the cognitive aspect of the process as including confirmation of the capacity for learning on the part of the students, ongoing assessment of student knowledge, and connected learning—that is, connecting to one another and connecting ideas to experience (1995).

Perkins, Jay, and Tishman point out that the context and

social dimension of thinking influences the process of thinking. "People frequently (perhaps all too frequently) puzzle out their problems by themselves. But thinking also occurs in social contexts in which people need to work together and honor and learn from one another's perspectives and arrive at satisfactory mutual resolutions" (1994, p. 76). Palmer addressed the issue of knowing and community and their connection to our pervasive culture: "Scholars now understand that knowing is a profoundly community act. . . . In order to know something, we depend on the consensus of the community in which we are rooted—a consensus so deep that we often draw upon it unconsciously" (1983, p. xv).

Not surprisingly, students also find it difficult to separate social processes from learning (Baxter Magolda 1992; Belenky et al. 1986; Kuh et al. 1991; Tinto, Russo, and Kadel 1994). In their study on out-of-class experiences, Terenzini et al. described this phenomenon through students' words:

> Most students interviewed at [Southwest Community College] were field sensitive learners, relying on extrinsic stimuli to facilitate learning. We heard comments like "learning takes place in classroom discussions," and "I learn more through classroom discussion than from lectures," and "real learning takes place in the patio area because somebody is always experiencing something that you want to experience, so they tell you about it." It's interesting and they want to share it with you. Other students said learning occurred at home, through tutoring and with "friends who know a little more than you," as well as "everywhere." A white student explained the kind of learning that takes place at the college's picnic tables: "Like when you're studying for an exam and you don't think you understand and you explain it to another student, and all of the sudden, click, you understand. That's when you really know you understand and you can do it" (1992, p. 30).

In their study of "Involving Colleges," Kuh, Schuh, and Whitt indicated that "most students perceive in-class and out-of-class experiences to be seamless. That is, what is learned during college [at these involving institutions] is not easily partitioned into courses, friendships, organizations, library work, laboratory assignments, recreational activities, and so on. Classrooms, laboratories, student living environments, and work settings all can provide powerful learning opportunities" (1991, p. 184).

It appears that students do not naturally separate social processes, cognitive processes, and learning. Instead, these elements have been separated by those who have studied them and those who have attempted to teach students by only focusing on cognitive processes. As higher-education professionals, we need to put into practice the fact that learning is, in part, a social process.

Cognitive and Emotional Processes
Issues related to affect and emotion were among the first elements to be carved away from a holistic view of human beings and their development. These internal states were essentially invisible to the eye and, therefore, perceived as unknowable. Eliminating a recognition of the role of emotion in learning had an inevitable impact on the learning process. In an eight-year study of American schools, Goodlad found, among other problems, a disturbing lack of positive emotions in the classroom (1984).

Given that emotions were first out, perhaps it is not surprising that they are last in. As behaviorism—the school of psychology focused only on observable behaviors—waned in the 1960s, researchers began to focus on the internal processes of cognition—how the mind registered and stored information. At the same time, however, emotions still were off-limits (Goleman 1995). It has only been during the last several decades that the study of emotion's influence on learning and development has been integrated with work on cognition and social processes. This came after many unsuccessful years of trying to study emotions through physiological measurement. Hastorf and Isen (1982) highlight the difficulty of dealing with affect and cognitive development.

> *The question of affect . . . has not received much attention in traditional cognitive psychology. . . . Affect is treated as a thing apart, a separate force, a spoiler, to otherwise lawful cognitive relationships. . . . It has promoted corollary views that usually cognition is unaffected by affect and motivation, that only strong (and perhaps negative) emotions influence cognition, and that somehow this influence is to interfere with a more*

basic and otherwise orderly process (1982, p. 5).

Only when it was accepted that feeling states and thinking states were virtually inseparable did research move away from segregating affect or attempting to physically measure emotions to concentrating instead on people's cognitions, perceptions of feelings, and mutual influence. "Cognitive processes themselves are presumed to be complexly constructed and dependent on affective, motivational/contextual, and concurrent cognitive factors" (Hastorf and Isen 1982, p. 6). Goleman describes the interrelatedness of feelings and intellect:

> *These two minds, the emotional and the rational, operate in tight harmony for the most part, intertwining their very different ways of knowing to guide us through the world. Ordinarily there is a balance between emotional and rational minds, with emotion feeding into and informing the operation of the rational mind, and the rational mind refining and sometimes vetoing the inputs of the emotions. . . . In many or most moments these minds are exquisitely coordinated; feelings are essential to thought, thought to feeling. . . . Feelings are indispensable for rational decisions; they point us in the proper direction, where dry logic can then be of best use* (1995, pp. 9, 28).

Definitions of desirable cognitive outcomes of a college education often contain affective elements. In fact, the American Philosophical Association "evolved a consensual description of critical thinking as purposeful, self-regulatory judgment involving the possession and deployment both of cognitive abilities and affective dispositions" (Ewell 1994, p. 4). One cannot effectively judge a student's ability to think critically without considering affective factors.

When studying cognitive development and learning, it is difficult to separate out the role affect plays because learning is facilitated or hampered by emotions, moods, and feelings (Boekaerts 1993). King and Baxter Magolda point out that how individuals construct knowledge and their use of knowledge is closely tied to their sense of self (1996, p. 166). In referring to student learning Gamson indicated that, "You have to get people to a point where they can feel it.

Then you have an opportunity for growth and development" (1991, p. 44). Piaget viewed emotions as "the energetic source on which the functioning of intelligence depends . . . [and] insisted on a constant interaction and dialectic between affectivity and intelligence (DeVries and Kohlberg 1987, p. 33). Piaget saw the affective and cognitive elements of development as inseparable, that "feelings are structured along with the structuring of knowledge" (p. 33).

Sylvester points out that emotion is important in education because it drives attention, which in turn drives learning and memory (1994). Memories formed during a specific emotional state tend to be easily recalled during a similar emotional state later on (Thayer 1989). "Classroom simulations and role-playing activities enhance learning because they tie memories to the kinds of emotional contexts in which they later will be used" (Sylvester 1994, p. 63). This type of learning activity may be less useful for traditional testing in that the emotional context of a written exam differs from that of simulations and role plays, but these activities may be more beneficial for real-life situations beyond the classroom in which the students will find themselves.

Emotions also affect motivation to learn. Depressed mood states often correlate with decreased motivation in the classroom (Peterson and Seligman 1984). "Students who are anxious, angry, or depressed don't learn; people who are caught in these states do not take in information efficiently or deal with it well" (Goleman 1995, p. 78). Bless, Bohner, Schwarz, and Stack (1990) found that individuals in a good mood are more likely to be persuaded in a learning or decision-making situation than those in a bad mood. However, their findings also suggested that the likelihood of effortful, analytic processing of information on the part of individuals may decrease as mood states become more positive. That is, the better and happier a person feels the less likely it is that he or she will subject incoming information to critical analysis and accept it on face value. The complex nature of these findings—a good mood is beneficial to learning, but perhaps it should not be too good—has significant implications for individuals trying to facilitate student learning. It warrants the attention of classroom faculty and other educators.

A student's development can be enhanced by actively bringing the dimensions of affect and cognition together. Ellis, the originator of Rational-Emotive Therapy, "believes that affect, behavior, and cognition interact with one another in intricate ways; however, he accords cognition a particularly influential position in these interactions and considers it a more convenient point of intervention than the other processes" (Barrow 1986, p. 15). Therefore, the intellectual work that occurs in college is an ideal avenue for assisting with students' affective development. Chickering and Reisser concur: "Assignments that invite students to engage emotionally as well as intellectually can assist them with the management of emotions, which must first be brought into awareness before they can be given powerful expression" (1993, p. 61). Page and Page discovered that goal-setting and problem-solving developed students' self-esteem by enhancing their perception of competence, another link between cognitive processes and affective development (1993).

There also is research on the impact of emotional skills and aptitudes on college outcomes. Goleman points out several studies in which emotional skills were better predictors of various measures of academic success than was IQ (1995). For example, in one study of 4-year-olds, those who were unable to delay gratification and control impulses in a simple experiment involving marshmallows had significantly lower SAT scores 14 years later than those who could wait for gratification. In the experiment each child received one marshmallow; if she could wait 15 minutes before eating it then she got two. The SATs showed a 210-point difference from an average of 1052 for those who could not wait to an average of 1262 for those who could.

In another study, a student's level of hope (that is, "believing you have both the will and the way to accomplish your goals" [Goleman 1995, p. 86]) was a better predictor of first-semester grades than were SATs. Finally, another study discovered that first-year students' scores on a test of optimism ("the strong expectation that, generally, things will turn out all right in life despite setbacks and frustrations" were better predictors of grades for the first year than were their SAT scores or their high-school grades [p. 88]). Goleman concludes that given about the same range of intellectual abilities, emotional skills and propensities (such as the ability to delay gratification, having hope, being optimistic) make the critical difference. The good news is that even in the face of claims that IQ scores cannot be raised by training, emotional abilities can. In turn, emotional abilities can enhance cognitive abilities and outcomes and academic achievement.

Research also supports the assumption that an emotionally positive classroom climate facilitates learning and therefore enhances students' academic achievement (Li 1992; Seiler 1989). Connell found that students in classrooms in which they have a sense of belonging or relatedness yielded higher scores on measures of perceived academic control (1990). Students who were emotionally secure with classmates and faculty were more likely to be active participants in class and exerted more effort in their work, thus maintaining and enhancing their academic achievement (Cabello and Terrell 1994; Tinto and Goodsell 1993). For at-risk students (students with lowered aspirations, low self-esteem, low internal locus of control, negative attitudes toward school, history of failure, fractured families, substance abuse), the single most frequent perception is that their teachers do not care about them, which in turn serves to block their cognitive and affective development (Kagan 1990).

Emotional and Social Processes
The importance of the connection and interplay between the affect and the social—and the difficulty in separating them—is represented in human-development research by the long tradition of psychosocial theories of development (Chickering 1969; Chickering and Reisser 1993; Erikson 1959; Kegan 1982; Loevinger 1976). More recently, Gardner, in his theory of multiple intelligences, includes interpersonal intelligence (1993). A person with a high degree of interpersonal intelligence is better able to perceive and respond appropriately to the moods, desires, and motivations of other people. Salovay and Mayer's model of Emotional Intelligence includes two social areas—recognizing emotions in others and managing relationships (1990).

There is a clear recognition of the strong connection between an individual's emotional and affective development and the social context, in that most emotions originate in social events (Smith-Lovin 1989). Shott (1979) described emotions as socially constructed and Smith-Lovin (1989) indicated that feelings always are interpreted in a social milieu—change the social milieu and most likely the feelings will change. Students who feel the discomfort associated with the challenge of learning will interpret that discomfort differently depending whether they are within a supportive social context, a competitive social context, or a context in which they feel marginalized and unimportant.

An individual's affective development also influences social understanding and interpersonal interactions. For example, Sommers reported that "the importance attached to heterosexual ties in young adulthood and the intense emotions that accompany such relationships in their initial development [may] interfere with the establishment of intimacy" (1982, p. 10). Students' processes of learning to manage their emotions will influence their willingness and ability to interact socially in and out of the classroom (Chickering and Reisser 1993).

The relationship between emotional states and social performance in the classroom is strong. In her study of classroom participation, Fassinger discovered that "faculty's greatest impact on class participation stems from course designs; for example, when professors create activities that foster positive emotional climates, they are likely to cultivate interactions. . . . A positive emotional climate can enhance the likelihood of class participation, particularly for females" (1995, pp. 93-94). Positive emotional climates were those characterized by students as supportive, where cooperation was the norm, and in which they could get to know other students and develop friendships. Fassinger also reports that activities related to developing a student's self-confidence (an affective state) will enhance their ability and willingness to participate in class discussions and activities (social process).

Emotional, Social, and Cognitive Processes
While the boundaries between any of these elements are blurred, the mutually reinforcing and developmentally influential nature of affective, social, and cognitive elements is clear. Pace concluded in his study of college student experiences that "good things go together" (1987, p. 1). That is, those who benefit most intellectually from the college experience also seem to benefit more in the affective- and social-development domains. He also found that students who devoted more time and energy to personal and social activities benefited more intellectually. Gardner pointed out that "the creation of cooperative, supportive environments in homes, schools, and communities has been shown to have a

positive effect on students' social and psychological well-being, which eventually leads to higher academic achievement" (1993, p. 244).

O'Keefe and Delia argue that the more cognitively complex people are, the more likely they will holistically perceive the situations and contexts in which they interact (1982). Baxter Magolda labeled the most advanced level of cognitive development contextual knowing, which integrates relational (social and affective) and impersonal (objective) knowing (1995). Good things do go together.

King and Baxter Magolda specify the interrelatedness of cognitive, social, and affective elements of development:

> *The qualities associated with a college-educated person include more than the cognitive ability to engage in critical thinking; they also include such affective attributes as an eagerness to continue to learn, an appreciation of the value of working with diverse others on problems of mutual interest, the will to take personal responsibility for one's views and actions, and the desire to make a positive contribution. . . . For example, effective conflict mediation can require not only a complex understanding of the underlying issues (cognitive complexity), but also the ability to open and continue a dialogue between disputing parties (interpersonal skills) and an understanding of the limits of one's role (personal maturity)* (1996, pp. 163-64).

It also must be noted that negative or dysfunctional elements within any of the three domains will negatively influence the other two. Palmer indicates that fear of conflict in teaching and learning leads both students and faculty away from developing communities, thereby reducing interpersonal interactions and intellectual development (1987). Positive emotional climates enhance the sense of community and also allow that community to work together toward mutual understanding and enhanced learning. As Palmer suggests:

> *What prevents [creative] conflict in our classrooms is a very simple emotion called fear. . . . It's fear of exposure, of appearing ignorant, or being ridiculed. And the only antidote to that fear is a hospitable environment created,*

for example, by a teacher who knows how to use every
remark, no matter how mistaken or seemingly stupid, to
upbuild both the individual and the group. . . . Com-
munity is precisely that place where an arena for cre-
ative conflict is protected by the compassionate fabric of
human caring itself (1987, p. 25).

Summary

Research is continuing to enhance our understanding of the interrelationships and mutually reinforcing nature of the intellectual, social, and emotional elements of student learning. What is most important is a recognition that they do interact and influence one another. Building on any single element has the potential to enhance the other two. On this research base and with the recognition of the interrelatedness of the elements of student learning, professionals can develop practices that incorporate each of these elements. To do so will move the college community toward a more closely integrated experience for students, one that affirms their intuitive sense of connectedness of affective, social, and cognitive processes. To disregard practices that incorporate each of these elements will reinforce the fragmentation among these elements and between students and faculty, student affairs professionals, and the institution. Individual practices and institutional strategies are explicated in the next two sections.

THE LINKS AMONG INTELLECTUAL, SOCIAL, AND EMOTIONAL ELEMENTS OF LEARNING: INDIVIDUAL ISSUES

Expanding the Notion of Learning

Throughout much of the history of higher education, learning has been assumed to take place in the classroom, be facilitated by faculty, and be focused on cognitive and intellectual development. Recent research is undermining these assumptions (Astin 1993; Kuh, Schuh, and Whitt 1991; Pascarella and Terenzini 1991). At colleges in which active involvement in and out of the classroom is fostered, students differentiate between in-class and out-of-class learning much less than assumed (Kuh et al. 1991). At all institutions, professionals and activities outside of the classroom influence student learning more than supposed (Astin 1993; Pascarella and Terenzini 1991).

Focusing solely on cognitive or intellectual development and ignoring social and emotional influences on the learning process reduces the effectiveness of teaching. Failing to recognize the intellectual and cognitive aspects of emotional and social issues allows teachable moments to pass unnoticed. Institutions and individuals must put into place actions that correspond with the emerging assumptions regarding the interrelatedness of cognitive, emotional, and social elements of learning. Present cultural norms and practices must be identified and, where appropriate, discarded, while new ones must be nurtured. Policies and practices must be implemented on our campuses that respond to what the research is discovering. In this and the following section, individual and institutional issues related to this expanded notion of learning are discussed and implications and suggestions are presented.

Interacting dimensions

In designing the conceptual framework for these sections, we came to recognize several interacting dimensions. These included the mutually shaping issues of one's personal philosophy and professional practice, the continuum of action from individual practices to institutional interventions, and the separate spheres of faculty, student affairs professionals, and the institution. We have attempted to incorporate each of these elements into the structure of the rest of this report. In this section we focus on individual issues because we believe that without individual transformation of philosophy and practice, institutional policies and actions will be empty, misguided, and ineffective.

The components of this section—liberation theory, constructivist pedagogy, critical cultural perspective, and collaborative learning—are philosophically based. In fact, each has many philosophical similarities and all have implications for practice. We have arranged them from most abstract to most concrete. This section focuses on individuals and concludes with implications for faculty and student affairs professionals. The next section focuses on institutional issues and implications.

Individual Philosophy, Practice, and Transformation
Traditional pedagogies, especially the dominance of and reliance upon lecture as the sole method of classroom instruction, clearly are under attack (Freire 1978; Giroux 1983; Schniedewind and Davidson 1987; Shor 1992). In their place have proliferated interrelated philosophies, pedagogies, and practices such as liberation theory (Freire 1970; McLaren and Leonard 1993; Shor 1992), constructivist pedagogy (Brooks and Brooks 1993), critical cultural perspective (Rhoads and Black 1995), and collaborative learning (Bruffee 1987, 1993; Gabelnick et al. 1990; Goodsell et al. 1992). We have chosen to focus on these practices because they challenge the traditional model of learning and because they acknowledge, address, and make use of social and emotional influences on learning. By changing the nature of authority in learning experiences or by bringing the personal experiences of students to bear on a topic, these practices hold tremendous potential for reshaping individual practice and, in turn, higher education. In the sections that follow we describe these practices and the outcomes and propose strategies for implementation.

Liberation theory
First articulated by Paulo Freire in his 1970 book *Pedagogy of the Oppressed*, liberation theory has been adopted and adapted by teachers at all levels of education in the United States. Freire's work also has been referred to as empowering education (Shor 1992) and critical pedagogy (Giroux 1988; McLaren 1989).

The work that led Freire to develop his theory involved the literacy movement among peasants in Brazil. As a teacher trying to transform people's lives through education, he discovered that the educational system actually continued the experience of oppression for these people. Rather than being a vehicle for changing society, Freire identified the education system as one of the major instruments for the maintenance of both the positive and negative aspects of the culture. Therefore, a basic premise of liberation theory is that society's cultural system perpetuates power relationships and holds people (and groups) in place like an invisible web. The strength and pervasiveness of cultural systems have been well-documented and, as explained earlier, a cultural perspective can be used to better understand our system of higher education. Freire argued that we must go beyond understanding the cultural system to transforming that system if we want education to be truly liberating and empowering.

Freire's most notable metaphor for traditional education is the banking model of education, in which students are viewed as empty vessels and the role of educators is to fill them with knowledge as one would fill a bank (1970). Freire argued that the educational system must be transformed through praxis. Praxis is "reflection and action upon the world to transform it" (Freire 1970, p. 36). Praxis goes beyond practice and action—two words at its root—in that it also requires critical reflection on practice and action. This critical reflection is on the beliefs, assumptions, norms, and practices that support and perpetuate the current cultural system. These include the ordinary, everyday actions that perpetuate the systems that separate the haves and have-nots in our educational system, such as what books are chosen for a course, who is called upon in class, with whom faculty and student affairs professionals spend time, and what topics are included in class and out-of-class discussions.

One element of praxis is critical dialogue among members of the system (in this case, faculty, student affairs professionals, and students). According to Freire, such a dialogue involves a profound trust that both educator and student are open to change. "From the outset, [the educator's] efforts must coincide with those of the students to engage in critical thinking and the quest for mutual humanization. [The educator's] efforts must be imbued with the profound trust in [people] and creative power. To achieve this, [the educator] must be a partner of the students" (p. 62).

As partners, educators and students critically examine their own existence, their roles in the education process, the subject matter, and the learning process. From a liberatory perspective, reflective practice reduces the status, power differences, and hierarchical distance between professionals

By changing the nature of authority in learning experiences or by bringing the personal experiences of students to bear on a topic, these practices hold tremendous potential for reshaping individual practice and, in turn, higher education.

and students. The professional becomes a teacher/student, while the student becomes a student/teacher. Everyone learns from everyone else.

The ultimate goal of education from a liberation theory perspective is the attainment of critical consciousness. One who has attained an advanced level of critical consciousness, to which Freire refers as critical transitivity, thinks holistically and critically, is personally empowered regarding his or her own education, and is aware of the influence of context and conditions on the learning process. People who operate from a critically transitive perspective recognize the existence, location, and use of power in various sectors of society; have developed advanced levels of critical thinking ability; recognize the influences of socialization on themselves and others; work to make conscious the process; and take part in and initiate social change projects (Shor 1993).

Using liberation theory as a basis for one's professional practice is not the same as trying a new strategy or technique. It requires a transformation of one's view of the teaching and learning process.

Transforming one's professional practice to incorporate the tenets of liberation theory necessarily incorporates the social and affective dimensions of learning into the educational process. The first two sets of values in a list of 11 Shor cites which underlie empowering education—his term for liberatory education—are participatory and affective (1992). Participation, partnership, and dialogue require that students and educators enter into a conscious relationship, complete with mutual expectations and responsibilities. Students are expected to take their own learning seriously and to contribute to the education of others (including the instructor). This type of pedagogy is highly participative in that it is through dialogue upon which students come to reflect, know, and build upon their own experience and knowledge.

Regarding emotions, Shor compared the differences between empowering education and traditional, teacher-centered competitive pedagogy.

In traditional classrooms, negative emotions are provoked in students . . . self-doubt, hostility, resentment, boredom, indignation, cynicism, disrespect, frustration, the desire to escape. . . . Negative feelings interfere with learning and lead to strong anti-intellectualism in

countless students. . . . In a participatory class where
authority is mutual, some of the positive affects which
support student learning include cooperativeness, curios-
ity, humor, hope, responsibility, respect, attentiveness,
openness, and concern for society (1992, pp. 23-24).

As pointed out earlier, Goleman presented powerful evidence of the academic achievement and cognitive development of students who exhibited high levels of hope,
optimism, and impulse control (1995). Allowing the tenets of
liberation theory to transform one's practice opens avenues
to more effectively use the affective elements of learning to
enhance holistic student learning.

This synopsis of Freire's work only begins to touch on its
complexity. Additionally, Freire's work continues to be
debated as its application spreads into higher education. For
example, Manning cites the Christian overtones in the work
and suggests that a more appropriate term for his work is
liberation theology (1994). In any case, liberation theory
with its focus on bringing students' emotional and social
experiences to bear on the learning process gives us powerful ideas for shaping our professional practice.

Constructivist pedagogy

Constructivist pedagogy entails many of the same underlying
assumptions as practice based upon liberation theory.
Constructivism defines knowledge as temporary, developmental, socially and culturally mediated, and thus nonobjective. Learning from this perspective is understood to be a
self-regulated process of resolving inner cognitive conflicts
that often become apparent through concrete experience,
collaborative discourse, and reflection (Brooks and Brooks
1993). Note the similar emphasis to liberation theory on
discourse (dialogue) and reflection (critical consciousness).
Constructivist pedagogy is dissimilar from liberation theory
in its lack of a conscious focus on social change and cultural
transformation. It is more clearly focused on the practices of
teaching and the processes of learning.

Constructivist pedagogy celebrates the complexity of the
known world rather than searching for ways to reduce it to
simple units and products. It is based upon the premise that
educators "must provide a learning environment in which
students search for meaning, appreciate uncertainty, and

---

inquire responsibly" (Jackson 1993, p. v). It recognizes that emphasis on performance and giving the right answers results in little long-term recall, whereas a focus upon learning results in greater long-term understanding and ability to use the concepts and information out of the classroom (Katz 1985). "The goals of constructivist pedagogy include helping students to take responsibility for their own learning, to be autonomous thinkers, to develop integrated understandings of concepts, and to pose—and seek to answer—important questions" (Brooks and Brooks 1993, p. 13).

Brooks and Brooks compare traditional classrooms and constructivist classrooms on a variety of dimensions.

TABLE 1
A LOOK AT SCHOOL ENVIRONMENTS

Traditional Classrooms	Constructivist Classrooms
Curriculum is presented part to whole, with emphasis on basic skills.	Students primarily work in groups.
Strict adherence to fixed curriculum is highly valued.	Pursuit of student questions is highly valued.
Curricular activities rely heavily on textbooks and workbooks.	Curricular activities rely heavily upon primary sources of data and manipulative materials.
Students are viewed as "blank slates" onto which information is etched by the teacher.	Students are viewed as thinkers with emerging theories about the world.
Teachers generally behave in a didactic manner, disseminating information to students.	Teachers generally behave in an interactive manner, mediating the environment for students.
Teachers seek the correct answer to validate student learning.	Teachers seek the students' point of view in order to understand students' present conceptions for use in subsequent lessons.
Assessment of student learning is viewed as separate from teaching and occurs almost entirely through testing.	Assessment of student learning is interwoven with teaching and occurs through teacher observations of students at work and through student exhibitions and portfolios.
Students primarily work alone.	Students primarily work in groups.

Constructivism refocuses on the interactionist aspect of Piaget's work that often is ignored by students of his research on cognitive development, in that knowledge comes neither from the focus of learning nor from the learner but from the interaction and unity of the two (Piaget and Inhelder 1971). Constructivist pedagogy requires a two-way conversation between educator and students as well as among students.

Emotional states are recognized as a vital aspect of enhancing learning through constructivist pedagogy. Piaget identified interest as a vital affective state in the process of knowledge construction among children (1969).

> *Without interest, the [student] would never make the constructive effort to make sense out of experience (that is, no assimilation to existing structures would occur). Without interest in what is new, the child would never modify the instrument of reasoning (that is, would make no accommodation of existing structures). Interest performs a regulatory function, freeing up or stopping the investment of energy in an object, person, or event. Thus, methods aimed at promoting this constructive process must arouse the child's spontaneous interest* (DeVries and Kohlberg 1987, p. 25).

Educators who operate from a constructivist perspective recognize the importance of interest, motivation, curiosity, intrigue, and inspiration in the learning process. They consciously construct activities that address both cognitive as well as affective states in students. This is accomplished in part by connecting current lessons to students' previous knowledge and personal experience. They recognize that motivation and interest also often are generated through interaction with one's peers, thus linking the social and affective process to enhance learning.

Constructivist educators also experience the resistance that countercultural activities bring.

> *Schools throughout America are filled with students . . . who have been acculturated to devalue thinking, to feel uneasy about in-depth analysis, and to view anything other than rapid coverage of the curriculum as wasting time. These students are frequently successful in school.*

They study, complete their assignments, pass their tests, and receive good grades. Yet, these are not meaningful victories. They are victories of form over substance, of superficiality over engagement, of coverage over depth (Brooks and Brooks 1993, pp. 119-20).

Furthermore, students and teachers may think that this process of constructing knowledge is all well and good for the humanities and social sciences but not for such hard topics as mathematics and the natural sciences. However, at the K-12 level, both the National Council for Teachers of Mathematics and the National Science Teachers Association have endorsed the underlying concepts of constructivist pedagogy and have recommended a move away from a focus on memorization and a quest for right answers and toward the processes used to obtain answers (Fosnot 1993).

Critical cultural perspective
In writing this report we have adopted a cultural perspective to help us understand how we have reached this point in history where students' lives and learning experiences have become so fragmented. The intellect has been divided away from emotions and then further dichotomized from the social lives and social development of students. This, in turn, has contributed to the relative lack of effectiveness of higher education in addressing issues of values and moral and ethical development.

Other dichotomies include the division of the classroom and the nonclassroom experiences of students. Student affairs professionals have little idea of what is going on inside the classrooms on their campuses and few faculty understand or are aware of what is going on outside the classroom in their students' lives (Love et al. 1993). It has been argued elsewhere that the path to holistic student development is through the joining of forces between faculty and student affairs professionals and by actively bridging the in-class and out-of-class experiences of students (Baldridge 1981; Miller and Jones 1991). We do not argue that these are inappropriate goals, we only suggest that they are incomplete. They perpetuate the current cultural systems and underlying assumptions that caused the dichotomization in the first place—the fragmentation of the intellectual, social, and affective experiences of students.

Adopting a critical cultural perspective goes beyond a cultural perspective in that the strength and embeddedness of the current culture and subcultures are recognized (Rhoads and Black 1995). This perspective requires that the underlying assumptions of our current system of higher education be identified, analyzed, and changed for effective and lasting change to occur regarding student learning and development. A critical cultural perspective "focuses attention upon the role teachers might play in creating democratic classrooms in which students struggle to understand how culture and social structure have shaped their lives " (Rhoads and Black 1995, p. 413). We not only must examine our assumptions and values as educators and how we put them into practice, but we must examine the assumptions and values that support and perpetuate our current fragmented educational system. Adopting a critical cultural perspective also involves some of the practices described in liberation theory and constructivist pedagogy.

The power and pervasiveness of the culture of higher education is taken as a given by most who consider it (Chaffee and Tierney 1988; Kuh and Whitt 1988). Early attempts at managing culture met with little success (Chaffee and Tierney 1988; Kuh and Whitt 1988; Schein 1985), mainly because the proponents attempted to manage culture through a rationalistic perspective (e.g., Kilmann, Saxton, and Serpa 1985; Wilkins and Patterson 1986). This treats culture as a commodity that can be planfully and willfully shaped and molded.

Some have given up trying to utilize a cultural perspective in organizational transformation; however, others recognize that managing culture is what all educators do (Manning 1993) and that effectively utilizing a cultural perspective in the transformation of higher-education organizations takes persistence, leadership, risk-taking, and tenacity (Roueche and Baker 1987; Schein 1985). Rhoads and Black compare a critical cultural perspective to liberation theory in that they see students, faculty, and student affairs professionals engaging "one another in mutual debate and discourse about issues of justice, freedom, and equality" (1995, p. 418).

Faculty and student affairs professionals who adopt liberation theory as an aspect of their teaching and professional philosophy will be unable to avoid adopting a critical cultural perspective (Manning 1994). They will be encouraged through dialogue with other faculty, student affairs professionals, and their students to examine the norms, values, expectations, and assumptions regarding their professional practice and their role in the institution.

Adopting a critical cultural perspective includes developing a recognition of how faculty and student affairs professionals "play a role in the way college and university communities are structured" (Rhoads and Black 1995, p. 418), especially in the way learning activities are structured. For example, the field of student affairs is involved in a discussion regarding its role in student learning, especially through dissemination of *The Student Learning Imperative* (American College Personnel Association 1994). As indicated previously, despite claims that a purpose of student affairs is to foster holistic student development (American Council on Education 1937, 1949; National Association of Student Personnel Administrators 1987), the field has, in fact, predominantly focused on issues of social and affective development.

Student affairs professionals are critically examining the role they have played in maintaining the fragmentation of the intellectual, social, and emotional elements of learning. This perspective also recognizes the role of the social setting on individual learning and development, the need to reduce power differentials throughout the learning process, and using conflict to enhance learning (Goleman 1995) and as an opportunity to transform the learning community (Rhoads and Black 1995).

A critical cultural perspective must pervade all that is done to facilitate an integrated notion of student learning. For example, the cultural differences between faculty and student affairs professionals must be brought to a conscious level as part of the process of promoting faculty-student affairs learning-based interaction. A critical cultural perspective is an element of each of the strategies, models, and implications presented in this report. Without a recognition of and respect for the power of the cultures that exist within the academy, efforts will be misguided and ineffective.

Another important task is identifying the cultural barriers that exist within ourselves (our assumptions, expectations, and beliefs) and those that exist within the other subcultures in higher education. For example, students may resist having other professionals address intellectual issues because it is counter to the prevailing culture. They also may resist having other students act in instructive ways, preferring instead the expert instructor (Shor 1992). Faculty members may tend to stay within their disciplinary subcultures, and administrators often feel lucky if they can leave their offices, let alone their familiar assumptions, beliefs, and actions. Overcoming this tendency to remain within one's own culture will take conscious action and persistence. It will take work to overcome the fear associated with risk, and it will require much face-to-face interaction to develop trust. The subsections that follow focus on the role of a critical cultural perspective in shaping one of the most important cultures influencing student learning—that of students.

Shaping student culture. Student culture must be shaped to enhance an emphasis on holistic learning. This is not to imply we advocate some sort of Machiavellian attempt to mold students and their culture into our vision of a perfect holistic learning environment. Efforts to shape student culture must begin with the recognition that on many of our campuses an anti-intellectual student culture exists that accepts and fosters the fragmentation of the intellectual, emotional, and social elements of learning. The next step is a desire to change this culture in partnership with students.

Student culture, the peer group, and peer interactions are social elements that profoundly influence the intellectual experiences of students. Enhancing the educational climate and promoting involvement (described in the next section) both will influence and shape the student culture on campus. However, given what appears to be a long history of anti-intellectualism among a majority of students (Horowitz 1987), other actions must be taken to influence and shape student culture to enhance the degree to which intellectual, social, and emotional experiences are integrated.

The peer group long has been recognized as one of the most, if not *the* most, powerful influence in students' collegiate experience (Astin 1977, 1993; Newcomb 1943; Newcomb and Wilson 1966; Pascarella and Terenzini 1991). Studies have concluded that positive peer group interactions contribute to persistence and success in college. However, shaping student culture is a significantly complex and challenging task about which much more needs to be known (Kuh 1995). One result of the fragmentation of the student learning experience is that much of student socialization to college has been abdicated to the peer group. At large universities adults are virtually nonexistent in the lives of students (Moffatt 1989). Faculty, student affairs professionals, and administrators are distant characters in the drama of students' collegiate experience.

Student culture needs to be shaped in ways that will enhance intellectually oriented peer interactions, promote academic-related activities (Kuh 1995), and encourage faculty-student interaction (Astin 1993; Bowen 1977; Chickering and Reisser 1993; Kuh 1995; Kuh, Schuh, and Whitt 1991; Pascarella and Terenzini 1991). Kuh indicated that "given the frequency with which students mentioned interactions with peers as antecedents to their learning, more research is needed on how to harness peer influence to further the educational aims of the institution (for example, nurturing student cultures that foster a high level of student involvement in educationally powerful activities)" (1995, p. 149). Higher-education professionals need to find ways to shape and use this power to enhance the mission of higher education—the holistic development of students. Higher-education professionals must become a more direct influence in the lives of students. Only by direct influence will we be able to enter into partnerships with students and counter some of the values and assumptions in the dominant peer group that are contrary to the mission of the institution.

Kuh indicated that "a key step in enhancing student learning outside the classroom is determining if the institution's ethos values holistic approaches to learning and student participation in all aspects of institutional life" (1995, p. 150). Institutions must be committed to making sure this ethos incorporates the student culture as well. Given that student culture is developed and spread through peer interaction one strategy for institutions is to make use of the power of the peer group by developing alternative intellectual-based peer group programs. These include ideas such as peer-led supplemental instruction programs (Lundeberg and Moch 1995) and freshman interest groups (Goodsell 1993), which are small groups of first-year students (about 20) who share several classes.

Faculty influence on shaping student culture. One of the concerns regarding experiences that integrate intellectual, social, and emotional elements of learning is that faculty tend not to have enough contact with students out of class. At larger institutions, they often do not have much contact with students in class, either. However, faculty can make use of the power of the peer group through actions in the classroom, thereby helping to help enhance student culture on campus in and out of class. Unfortunately, the classroom remains a significant, though often disconnected, place in students' lives (Moffatt 1989). Faculty need to recognize their ability to connect what students learn in the classroom with their experiences beyond the classroom. Alternative pedagogies (such as liberation theory and constructivist pedagogy) encourage this type of connection, for example, by trying to use student experience as a starting point for learning.

Faculty need to recognize their ability to connect what students learn in the classroom with their experiences beyond the classroom.

Another way faculty can influence student culture is to identify and bring to conscious level the tacit understandings of student culture and work to change some of the questionable cultural elements surrounding academic work (Love 1990). For example, cultural norms have focused almost solely upon individual work and competition. This can be disrupted in many ways by faculty but must be done consciously, because students have had many years in which these norms have been so ingrained that to deviate from them feels like cheating. Peer feedback on writing assignments is one example in which students may think that getting help means that it is not their work. Faculty need to identify the practices in their classroom that perpetuate these norms, assumptions, and values. Many of the practices in alternative pedagogies seem countercultural to both instructors and students. These include expecting student participation and critical reflection, utilizing peer leaders in class, assigning group projects, and developing in-class learning communities.

If the barriers between faculty and student are to be bridged outside the classroom, they first must be bridged inside. This has both social and emotional elements. Socially, it establishes a relationship between the instructor and the student, which can enhance an experience of connected knowing on the part of the student (Belenky et al. 1986). Emotionally, it gives an instructor knowledge of the wide variety of stresses and emotionally charged experiences students carry with them. Only by focusing on the individual student is it possible for faculty to tap into how the norms and values of the student culture related to learning are being enacted in and out of the classroom. By focusing on the individual student, faculty are stepping into a void that often is entered only by other students. Making connections with individual students provides alternative options to the environmental pressures they are experiencing in an often-anti-intellectual peer climate.

Student affairs professionals' influence on shaping student culture. Given their wider variety of organizational tasks, often-closer physical proximity to and extended contact with students, student affairs professionals have many different opportunities and a wider variety of interventions than faculty when it comes to using the power of the peer group to enhance holistic student learning. Some of the ways in which individual student affairs professionals can shape student culture are similar to those for faculty—by focusing on the individual student, encouraging contact with faculty, and intending to be an intellectual presence in students' lives. One example of this is by promoting academically related activities. Academically related activities are class-related activities that take place outside of class—applying classroom knowledge to other experiences, independent research projects, and attending academic symposia and programs, for example (Kuh 1995).

Student affairs professionals, through their roles as managers, supervisors, advisors, and counselors, often already are social and emotional presences in students' lives. By bringing intellectual elements to their work, student affairs professionals can role-model for students a more holistic professional presence. Student affairs professionals also must go beyond promoting academically related activities to participating in them. Promotion without participation can be viewed as lip service. Going and becoming actively involved (co-facilitating classes and seminars, for example) sends a much clearer message.

Other ways in which student affairs can influence student culture are through the organizational activities of admissions, new student orientation, academic advising, leadership training, and career planning and placement. Student affairs professionals must come to know the cultural values, beliefs, and assumptions they hold that relate to holistic student learning, create opportunities for wider expression among students and their groups of values related to the intellectual nature of students' experience, consciously "design interventions . . . that symbolize desired behavior and institutional values" (Manning 1993), assess changes, and persist in efforts to influence student culture.

Collaborative learning

Collaborative learning* is a broad term for a variety of educational strategies that encourage students and educators to work together actively, sharing the responsibilities of teaching and learning. Instead of focusing on the educator as the sole authority, students play a significant role in integrating the course information with their personal experiences, thereby becoming the authorities on how the course material relates to their present world. Collaborative learning actively incorporates social and affective dynamics between students, and between students and faculty, to enhance intellectual development and learning. As the name implies, collaborative learning strategies often incorporate the use of small groups of students working toward a common educational goal such as study groups preparing for an exam or pairs of students giving each other feedback on their writing.

The primary aim of collaborative learning strategies is to actively involve students in the learning process. They pay attention to the elements of peer support and interaction. Indeed, by acknowledging that students can learn from one another, collaborative learning strategies strive to harness the potential influence of the peer group and, in turn, assist in the shaping of student culture. In collaborative learning, emphasis is placed as much on the experiences students bring with them (the social context) as on the information disseminated in class (Johnson, Johnson, and Smith 1991; Smith and MacGregor 1992).

Collaborative learning promotes the idea that acquiring and creating knowledge is an active social process students need to practice, not a process in which students are spectators sitting passively in a lecture hall (Bruffee 1984, 1993). In

*Although we refer to collaborative learning throughout this section, it should be noted that cooperative learning is a similar pedagogical practice. It is beyond the scope of this report to elaborate on the similarities and differences between collaborative and cooperative learning. Instead, we refer these readers to Matthews, Cooper, Davidson, and Hawkes (1995) for a discussion of these ideas.

some ways collaborative learning is a practical extension of constructivist pedagogy in that it involves students constructing information by taking the material from the professor and critically examining it in light of their individual and collective knowledge base. Students are expected to help each other. This gives the professor the freedom to adjust his or her role to that of a task setter, classroom manager, or synthesizer instead of expert, director, and producer (Weiner 1986). Collaborative learning differs from traditional learning strategies in that the latter assumes one-way communication, from the professor to the student, whereas collaborative learning strategies recognize that students need to speak about their own ideas to try them out, practice them, and refine them; communication in collaborative settings becomes two-way (Bouton and Garth 1983).

The result of such intellectual and social involvement on the part of students is enhanced academic achievement (Astin 1985; Johnson et al. 1981; MacGregor 1991; Slavin 1989-90). Besides increases in achievement and involvement, social benefits of the use of collaborative learning strategies include developing interpersonal-communications skills and promoting positive relations between people of different ethnic backgrounds, while emotional benefits include promoting student self-esteem (Cuseo 1991; Ziegler 1981). Students report that they prefer collaborative types of instruction and gain greater motivation and interest in education in general (Cooper and Mueck 1990; Kohn 1986). Rosen identified social, affective, and cognitive influences of collaborative learning (1992).

The influences on students' cognitive development include increased long-term retention, development of higher-level thinking skills, and the ability to cater to a variety of learning styles. The influences on students' affective development include increased feelings of success, enjoyment of the learning process, and self-esteem. Social benefits include learning to cooperate with peers and accept other points of view and developing communication, negotiation, and leadership skills.

Collaborative learning strategies are examples of how students' social and emotional needs and processes can be used as catalysts for greater cognitive development. These strategies make use of the influence of student peer groups on individuals and do so within the context of an academic program. Therefore, they may enable students to satisfy their social needs and concerns while addressing their intellectual development. Rather than asking students to choose between one or the other, collaborative learning strategies seek to balance the intellectual, social, and emotional needs of students. In doing so, they allow a synergy to develop that can empower students to find that their whole college experience is greater than the sum of its parts.

It should be noted that while collaborative learning strategies have been shown to benefit all students, students at remedial levels of study show gains that are similar to or better than students who do not take developmental level courses (Tinto, Goodsell Love, and Russo 1994). Furthermore, collaborative learning strategies promote student involvement and achievement in settings in which such involvement is not easily attained. At commuter colleges and universities, students find support among their learning community peers that enables them to manage the many struggles they face simply getting to college, while also enhancing their involvement in the academic life of the institution (Russo 1995). As the numbers of students who commute to college and who need developmental courses rise, institutions must find ways to support their efforts. Collaborative learning strategies can do much to enhance their intellectual growth while meeting their social and emotional needs.

The benefits of collaborative learning for students have been presented above. The benefits for faculty members are equally important, especially if it is hoped that the enhancement of students' intellectual development through social and emotional processes will proliferate throughout higher education. Collaborative learning strategies appeal to faculty members who are seeking ways to remove themselves from center stage in the classroom. Faculty who are dissatisfied with traditional lecture and discussion methods or who have experienced the synergy of collaborative learning for themselves may look for opportunities to try something new. These faculty may be convinced of the benefit of these learning strategies for students, but unless they are given institutional support in their efforts to change their teaching style they may not persist. Faculty who are supported in their use of collaborative or cooperative techniques report immense gratification in being able to focus on new ways of teaching and in seeing their students respond. One faculty member at Seattle Central Community College said:

Meeting other faculty in a context of discussing teaching is exhilarating. I'm more enthused about teaching than I've been in years and it's all about rediscovering myself as a learner. . . . I've learned again something that I knew long ago as an undergraduate: I enjoy learning for its own sake. It makes you feel good and alive. Working with other faculty has been the key to this awakening (Gabelnick, MacGregor, Matthews, and Smith 1990, p. 82).

The importance of preparing for a collaborative classroom assignment cannot be overemphasized. Preparation of a well-designed assignment takes time, as should the preparation of a well-delivered lecture. It requires a thorough knowledge of one's students (for assigning group members or selecting the level of the task), knowledge of collaborative and cooperative learning strategies so an effective strategy can be chosen, and knowledge of the topic. Since most effective strategies result in a finished product other than answers on an objective test, time must be spent reviewing and evaluating students' work. If this type of time devoted to improving the processes of teaching and learning is not valued and rewarded by the institution, then it is unlikely that faculty will continue to do it.

For professors to be rewarded, evaluation of their teaching must reflect an understanding of what a successful collaborative learning classroom looks and sounds like (Weiner 1986). Judged according to traditional teaching criteria, collaborative classrooms may appear unruly, loud, and disorganized. Evaluation needs to account for whether students' tasks are well-structured by the professor, students are sharing tasks and information, and opportunities exist for integration of material, to name a few examples.

The best resource about collaborative learning is Bruffee (1993); two other sourcebooks that bring together much useful information on this topic are Goodsell, Maher, Tinto, Smith, and MacGregor (1992) and Kadel and Keehner (1994). In addition, much has been written about active learning, a term that includes various classroom strategies such as small group discussions, case study methods, role-playing methods, and writing in class. For more information about strategies that can be employed in individual classes, we recommend three comprehensive sources: *Active*

Learning: Creating Excitement in the Classroom (Bonwell and Eison 1991), *Teaching College Freshmen* (Erickson and Strommer 1991), and *Promoting Active Learning: Strategies for the College Classroom* (Meyers and Jones 1993).

Implications
This section presents general implications of the concepts discussed as well as those specifically for faculty and student affairs professionals. Perhaps the most significant implication for individual faculty and student affairs professionals is that incorporating aspects of liberation theory, constructivist pedagogy, critical cultural perspectives, or collaborative learning into their professional practice will, in most cases, result in a personal transformation.

It is important to recognize that as we attempt to change the culture of the learning process, we as educators will change as well. To most effectively utilize the links among the intellectual, social, and emotional elements of learning, educators will need to more holistically present themselves to students. Student affairs professionals will need to exhibit more effectively to students the intellectual bases of their work and show themselves to be concerned about the cognitive elements of students' experience. Faculty will need to be seen as emotional and social beings. They must exhibit the passion they feel for their work, describe their frustrations and joys of learning, and show students they care about them and their learning. They must demonstrate the link between their social skills and the intellectual process through dialogue, mutually affirming interactions, and a recognition of student life beyond the classroom.

General implications
As indicated above, for most faculty and student affairs professionals adopting liberation theory, constructivist pedagogy, a critical cultural perspective, or collaborative learning as a professional philosophy and strategy is not merely adding additional techniques to one's repertoire. It often involves significant reflection, self-discovery, and transformation. For example, some of the actions[†] of adopting liberation theory or constructivist pedagogy include:

---

†Some of the ideas and material from this section came from discussions with Kathleen Manning, University of Vermont.

1. Do "with" students rather than doing "for" students (Manning 1994). Doing with students is at the heart of reducing status and power differences in the teaching/ learning relationship and creating partnerships with students. It requires that an educator see oneself as a fellow student (though not blind to one's authority), open to learning, open to the social influence of students and their groups, and aware of the affective elements of learning. This requires entering into a dialogue with students in which a trusting partnership as equal participants is established. It also involves trusting that students can succeed without overdirection by administrators and faculty.

2. Dismantle barriers to student learning. It is not absolutely necessary that faculty and student affairs professionals be doing more to enhance the teaching/learning process. In fact, there can be addition by subtraction, in that by dismantling barriers to student success such as recognizing and dealing with emotional impediments to learning, breaking down social barriers between and among students, and challenging current student cultural norms regarding the teaching/learning process, faculty and student affairs professionals can enhance the effectiveness of their teaching/learning practices.

3. Reflect on one's own socialization. Both faculty and student affairs professionals must reflect on their own cultural norms, values, expectations, assumptions, and beliefs *and* how they came to own them. One can start this process by reflecting on one's own undergraduate experience (both in and out of the classroom), the relationships with people who influenced one's attitudes toward academics and learning, one's graduate preparation, the social influence of others (fellow students, family, faculty, and student affairs professionals, for example), and the role of affect and emotion in their pursuit of their career.

4. Reflect on the practices that maintain the status and power differences between students and faculty and students and administrators, then work to reduce them.

   Professionals communicate expected differences in power and status through a variety of means—titles, clothes, demeanor, office/classroom furniture arrangement, interpersonal expectations, organizational hierarchies. A theme for a number of the "involving colleges"

(Kuh et al. 1991) was reduction or elimination in the use of titles (such as Professor, Mr., Ms., President, Dr.) without a reduction in mutual respect experienced by faculty, staff, or students. Rhoads and Black argue for minimizing organizational hierarchies to enhance the inclusiveness of our educational organizations (1995). If educators are interested in creating democratic learning environments and entering into a partnership with students in the learning process, then we need to explore the subtle and not so subtle ways in which we hold students at a distance through symbols of differential power and status.

5. Become culturally sensitive educators. One starts this process by gaining cultural knowledge as a means to critically reflect on one's own current reality and socialization. It also involves encouraging students and colleagues to explore cultural and societal assumptions, expectations, and context through dialogue and critically reflecting on those assumptions and expectations. This includes exploring cultural norms, assumptions, and behaviors of individuals and groups (racial and ethnic minority students, gay/lesbian/bisexual students, and students with disabilities, for example) different from the dominant cultural group in the institution—typically white, heterosexual, without disabilities—and reflecting on how these differing norms and expectations come into play in the teaching/learning process (Rhoads and Black 1995).

6. Teach the art of praxis. The first step of teaching the art of praxis is to ask students to reflect on their learning. This is a precursor to any meta-analysis of thoughts or feelings and often is absent in traditional teaching situations. Additional elements of praxis exist in critical thinking skills, in the skills of emotional intelligence (including self-awareness, managing emotions, recognizing emotions in others, handling relationships [Goleman 1995]), in adopting a critical cultural perspective, and even in leadership skills. These reflect higher order processes of metacognition (thinking about our thinking) and its emotional equivalent of self-awareness (an awareness of our feelings). Teaching the art of praxis goes beyond these by asking students to critically reflect on their often-subconscious cultural beliefs, behaviors, and assumptions and act to transform their own world—something of a meta-

acculturation (thinking about acculturation) combined with action.

7. Recognize and deal with student distrust of changes. Another important implication is that given the long history of the culture of higher education and the norms, values, assumptions, expectations, and behaviors that have been ingrained into students during their many years in this educational system, educators who begin the process of transforming their professional practice can expect significant resistance and distrust from their students. Practices that are countercultural will be resisted because of the fear they engender (Palmer 1990).

There are, of course, conflicts in empowering classrooms, chiefly among students with different values and needs, and between students and the teacher in the negotiation of meaning and requirements. In addition, the participatory class can also provoke anxiety and defensiveness in some students because it is . . . unfamiliar (Shor 1992, p. 25).

Students have internalized the cultural system (Freire 1970). Transformation to an empowering, liberatory, or constructivist educational practice requires trust, persistence, and confidence in the ultimate outcome. Freire also argues that it takes acts of profound love for those who benefit most from the system to work to dismantle and transform it.

Implications for faculty

The faculty facing the largest challenges and barriers to integrating intellectual, social, and emotional elements of learning are those who work at large four-year research universities, due to larger classes and more emphasis on scholarship and research. When looking for strategies to assist with integrating these elements we can turn to various exemplars of practice. These include involving colleges and community colleges (Kuh et al. 1991). Although the histories, cultures, and structures of community colleges differ radically from most four-year institutions, they still can be the source of valuable information.

In a sense, community colleges cannot do what four-year residential institutions do—that is, dichotomize students' experiences as in-class and out-of-class. Unlike their residential counterparts, community college students spend most of their time on campus in the classroom. If integration is going to happen, it most likely is going to happen there. Roueche and Baker studied Miami-Dade Community College, an exemplary community college as determined by a panel of national community college leaders and scholars (1987). Their findings revealed that the excellent faculty at Miami-Dade clearly integrated intellectual, social, and affective dimensions in their work. In fact, it was due in large measure to the fact that they integrated these elements that they were cited as excellent instructors. Roueche and Baker identified three major categories of instructional competencies exhibited by excellent instructors at Miami-Dade: motivational, interpersonal, and intellectual. Respectively, these represent the affective, social, and cognitive elements of the teaching/learning process.

. . . [faculty] having high expectations of students results in higher self-esteem and a higher self-concept concerning ability.

These instructors paid attention to the affective dimension of both student learning *and* their teaching. As faculty, they had high expectations of themselves as well as their students. They saw themselves as a motivating force behind students' good performance. They manifested a powerfully positive attitude which both challenged and inspired their students to achieve. They acted with compassion, understanding, a spirit of adventure, enthusiasm, and excitement (Roueche and Baker 1987). They also had high expectations for their students and provided the appropriate support for students to reach those expectations. Medley pointed out that having high expectations of students results in higher self-esteem and a higher self-concept concerning ability (1979). These excellent faculty sought to foster good attitudes in students and recognized and accepted that students brought emotions and feelings into the classroom and to their learning. Furthermore, because community colleges frequently have a wealth of cultural diversity in their student body, effective faculty encouraged students to bring their experiences into the classroom and contribute their knowledge to the topic. By doing this students not only became involved in classes, but they did not have to struggle as much with the clash of cultures that occurred between students, their families, and attendance at college (Rendon 1992). Excellent faculty utilized this additional information to better serve those students. Roueche and Baker cite one such professor: "I never discourage students who want to share personal feelings. This type of sharing often gives me insight as to the best approach to helping that student succeed" (1987, p. 162).

These instructors knew that students needed to feel accepted and cared about and they took a personal interest in their students (Roueche and Roueche 1994). They were committed to careful and distinct listening and attended to the nonverbal cues that provided them insight about their students. They actively sought personal information about their students, to notice them and to establish themselves as a presence in their students' lives. The purpose of this was to let the students know that they cared about them. This was true even for those instructors who taught large lecture classes (Roueche and Baker 1987).

Effective community college faculty also created a classroom social climate that was relaxed, comfortable, cheerful, friendly, nonthreatening, and positive (Easton 1983). Interpersonally, the Miami-Dade instructors had the ability to maintain an approving and mutually favorable relationship with students. They also facilitated these types of relationships among students to create a supportive and nonthreatening climate beneficial to student learning (Roueche and Baker 1987).

These faculty realized the interaction between the social and affective dimensions of the learning process.

> *A supportive climate prevents emotional overload by defining personal decorum. By sharing personal feelings, the teacher encourages the student to open up. When students do contribute, their information is put in the context of the lesson. The student is thus shown appreciation for his involvement, and the exchange models for other student that opinions, thoughts, feelings, and interests are accepted and respected in the classroom* (Roueche and Baker 1987, p. 158).

Excellent instructors also recognize what Murphy et al. discovered—that satisfying human relationships are a necessary but insufficient condition for student learning (1982). The excellent faculty at Miami-Dade used emotions and interpersonal relationships to get at their teaching missions but recognized that they were not substitutes for the teaching/learning process (Roueche and Baker 1987). The excellent faculty had effective teaching strategies, including well-organized courses, a focus on developing higher order thinking skills, relevant application of material, providing continuous feedback, and using a variety of delivery styles. They knew their subject matter, constantly integrated new ideas, sought out new strategies, and took risks to improve their curricula (Roueche and Baker 1987).

Excellent instructors had what Roueche and Baker termed an integrated perception of their students (1987). This was a holistic view both of their students and their subject matter. "Students are seen as whole individuals operating in a broader context beyond the classroom" (p. 152). They saw the students as more than just students and wanted them to integrate the material with subject matter of other classes.

Focusing on all colleges and universities, Chickering and Gamson outlined what they found to be the Seven Practices for Good Practice in Undergraduate Education (1987). These include such actions as encouraging contacts between students and faculty, respecting diverse talents and ways of learning, using active learning techniques, emphasizing time on task, and developing reciprocity and cooperation among students. Certainly, adopting those practices and those listed previously go a long way toward integrating cognitive, social, and affective dimensions of student learning. Additional strategies and implications include:

1. Assess social and emotional influences on the learning process and social and emotional outcomes of that process. Just as an instructor is interested in what a student knows about a particular topic before teaching it and then again afterward to see what the student has learned, assessing potential social and emotional influences before and social and emotional outcomes afterward are important aspects facilitating holistic student learning. The use of structured reflective journals allows faculty to be aware of the social and emotional issues students are bringing with them into the classroom. Other ideas include structured and open-ended questionnaires and self-reports. The use of such strategies also encourages students to connect what they are learning to their own experience. This may be easiest for most of the humanities and social sciences. However, as Lundeberg and Diemert Moch (1995) and Buerck (1985) discovered, it also is possible with the natural sciences and mathematics.

Faculty need to be interested and intentional about wanting to discover the impact of emotions on their students' performance. Students' negative reports regarding group work could be due to underdeveloped social skills or prior negative experiences with group work in class settings. Effective use of these strategies must be accompanied by faculty learning more about the psychosocial development of students.

2. Incorporate social and emotional elements in the teaching process. Chickering and Reisser make the point that intellectual activity is an effective avenue to incorporate work on social and emotional development (1993). An example is to have students include a section in their written work (e.g., research papers) on the impact of this learning on them and how it relates to their lives. As indicated above, faculty also should actively connect student experience to course material and the process of learning, expect and encourage questions and discussion, engage students in dialogue—individually and in groups, and identify barriers to learning (e.g., negative emotions and experiences and inadequate interpersonal skills). Enhancing social and emotional skills in turn enhances cognitive development and learning (Goleman 1995). Therefore, it makes sense to assess social and affective outcomes in course assignments and the course itself. These outcomes include items such as leadership skills, critical thinking, personal reflection, problem solving, teamwork, communication skills, and negotiation skills.

3. Focus on the individual student. Large lecture courses are an unpleasant reality of modern higher education, especially at large research universities. That setting makes it nearly impossible for faculty to focus on the individual student. However, not all classes are large lecture classes. Specific strategies to assist faculty in focusing on the individual student and to communicate an openness to the social and affective elements of their lives include the following:

■ **Learn students' names and something about them.** Isolation contributes to the development of groups with strongly held values and attitudes. Communicative isolation is more influential than physical isolation in modifying behavior (Newcomb and Wilson 1966). "Therefore, breaking down the isolation between two groups or subcultures . . . may modify attitudes and norms that, in turn, may change the differences between the two groups" (Love, Boschini, Jacobs, Hardy, and Kuh 1993, p. 72). In this case the isolation is between faculty and students. So, when faculty communicate with students and learn something about them it is the first step in destroying the anonymity and isolation that many students experience in their classes. In many cases—especially in larger lecture classes—this may take planning and work. One method is to have students use simple name tents made from index cards on their desks.

The results of a simply structured questionnaire distributed at the beginning of class can add texture to the two-dimensional faces that stare from the seats on the first day of class. Why are they there? What experience do they have with this subject? What do they expect to get out of the class, other than a grade? Knowing something about one's students can further sensitize oneself to the influences of social development and emotional issues on their class performance.

■ **Intend to become a presence in students' lives.**
Students may complain about their anonymity or the fact that their faculty do not know anything about them, but there also is safety in merely being a face in a crowd. Intentions are a powerful first step to integrating social and affective elements into the classroom. Faculty should let students know that they intend to get to know them. This needs to be established at the beginning of the term. Otherwise, students may be taken by surprise and resist, since faculty intending to get to know students often runs counter to the prevailing culture. Students should know faculty expectations in this area—that they intend to integrate intellectual, social, and affective elements of student experience.

■ **Encourage out-of-class student-faculty contact.** Part of the problem with encouraging out-of-class contact is that it often is the most successful and comfortable student who takes instructors up on their invitation to talk outside of class. Systematically meeting with small groups of students to assess their experience can bring faculty into closer contact with those anonymous students who often are in most need of connecting with institutional agents (Tinto 1993).

4. Reflect on your relationship with students and on the role social and emotional elements play in your teaching. The following questions suggest topics for reflection and basic actions faculty can take in this regard:

- How might you use office hours as an opportunity to talk with students informally about their experience in college as well as in the class, to get to know them as individuals, and help them to connect course material to their life?
- How often do you eat in the student center or dining hall or participate in campus activities, so students see you out of class and can approach you?
- How do you encourage students in your classes to get to know each other (by exchanging names and phone numbers, for example) and work together? As simple as this sounds, in large lecture classes students may never talk to the people around them (Goodsell 1993), thus contributing to an impersonal classroom and campus atmosphere.
- How often do you take your students out of the classroom, such as to the library, a museum, a theatrical performance on campus, or to hear a speaker?
- In what ways can you let students know how you came to pursue a career in your particular discipline, the role others played in the development of your career, and the role of motivation and commitment in attaining your position?

The answers to these questions can begin to peel away the layers of cultural assumptions and expectations that develop throughout a career. Discomfort with these questions is an indication of how closely we hold our cultural norms, yet this discomfort must be faced and overcome if real change is to occur. To expand our notion of learning may challenge some of our most valued beliefs, and that is what it may take to make holistic student learning a priority in higher education.

Implications for student affairs professionals

Although operating for the most part out of the classroom, Manning argues that student affairs professionals should adopt liberation theory as a professional philosophy:

> *Student affairs administrators, acting as supervisors, managers, and decision makers, maintain and recreate institutional structure. . . . Institutional transformation begins with individual critical consciousness.*

*Through a critical perspective on the power imbalances
and inequities of a particular system or institution,
people question and are empowered to change these
systems. Praxis, individual critical consciousness, and
transformation can serve as underlying assumptions or
premises of student affairs* (1994, pp. 94-95).

Student affairs professionals' most important action is the
need to incorporate learning with their notions of social and
affective development. Among the strategies and actions
they can take are assessing intellectual and cognitive development as part of out-of-class experiences, applying the
Seven Principles for Good Practice in Undergraduate
Education to aspects of their work, and being an intellectual
presence in the lives of their students.

**1. Assess intellectual and cognitive development as part
of out-of-class experiences.** Along with administrators and
faculty, student affairs professionals are struggling to assess
student outcomes. Given the history and culture of the field,
the tendency will be to focus efforts on assessing social and
emotional outcomes. To foster holistic student learning,
efforts must be expanded to include assessment of cognitive
outcomes as well. Rather than creating new assessment initiatives, student affairs professionals might look to current
assessment efforts and expand them to include elements of
intellectual development. Examples of efforts include
quality-of-life surveys in residence halls, student development transcripts, student satisfaction surveys, and evaluation
of service learning activities.

**2. Apply the Seven Principles of Good Practice in
Undergraduate Education** (Chickering and Gamson 1987).
Blimling and Alschuler provide examples of how student
affairs professionals can apply the principles of good practice in their work with students (1996). They suggest that
student affairs professionals can:

a. Encourage student-faculty contact through living learning centers, as advisors to student organizations, and include
faculty on student committees and other student groups,
such as intramurals.

b. Encourage cooperation among students through student government, residence hall associations, student organi-

zations, and the creation of democratic (Crookston 1974) and just (Kohlberg 1975) communities.

c. Encourage active learning through intramurals, outdoor education programs, student union boards, leadership training, retreats, peer advisor training, and service learning.

d. Give prompt feedback through disciplinary counseling, individual and group counseling, advising student organizations, and supervision of paraprofessionals.

e. Emphasize time on task through workshops on study skills, test taking, time management, and career planning.

f. Communicate high expectations through departmental publications, orientation and freshman seminars, leadership training, and recognition and award ceremonies.

g. Respect diverse talents through multicultural programming, development and support for special services and organizations for underrepresented groups, and support for pluralistic communities.

3. Be an intentional presence in students' intellectual lives. As Freire points out, everyday actions (and nonactions) serve to perpetuate cultural systems (1970). It has been recommended that student affairs professionals reflect on and critically analyze how they are perpetuating and how they can help dismantle the current culture that encourages the fragmentation of students' learning experiences.

Questions to help with this reflection are:

- How and when do you inquire about your students' studies and academic progress?
- How do you formally and informally promote good study habits among your students?
- How do you help students connect what they are learning in the classroom with their out-of-class experience?
- How do you encourage study groups, study time, or confront students who appear to be overly involved in social activities to the detriment of their studies?
- How do you know which students are succeeding academically and which students are struggling? What do you do?
- In what ways do you confront or promote the anti-intellectual culture that pervades many institutions?

It also is important to help students integrate social and emotional elements into their academic experience:

- How do you generate positive emotions about learning, studying, and academic pursuits?
- How do you promote intellectual and academic-based social interaction?
- How do you promote or diminish students' enthusiasm about learning?

As with the questions for faculty, these questions may create some discomfort among student affairs professionals. In addition, many student affairs professionals, such as those in registration, financial aid, or admissions, may believe these questions do not apply to them. The discussion that such unease may produce is sure to be important in the furthering of our understanding of the roles expected of student affairs professionals and the underlying beliefs of the profession.

Summary

Practices that integrate intellectual, social, and emotional elements of student learning cover a wide range of activities. Both faculty and student affairs professionals have roles to play in the process of integration. These roles must be played consciously and intentionally. A first step is reflecting on one's own philosophy and integrating these elements in our own minds as we transform our practice. In the next section we address institutional issues related to integrating intellectual, social, and emotional elements of learning.

THE LINKS AMONG INTELLECTUAL, SOCIAL, AND EMOTIONAL ELEMENTS OF LEARNING: INSTITUTIONAL IMPLICATIONS

American higher education is under a great deal of strain. External pressures and demands have intensified during the last two decades. For example:

Financial pressures are increasing—federal money is decreasing; state funds are diminishing; costs continue to rise, putting pressure on tuition; and students increasingly finance their education through loans.

Accountability demands are increasing—parents and students want to know what they are getting for their money; states are demanding increased outcomes assessment; states are boosting pressure to increase faculty time in the classroom; and the value of research is being questioned.

Student pressures are increasing—greater numbers of underprepared students are beginning higher education; more students must work longer hours to finance their education; more students of various cultural backgrounds are entering higher education; and more students with emotional, learning, and physical disabilities are entering higher education.

Faculty pressures are increasing—demands for research and productivity have remained constant while less research money is available and demands for increased teaching loads have intensified.

These external demands and internal pressures either have been resisted or assimilated into the current structures of academe. They also may be creating a context in which higher education has an opportunity to transform itself.

Self-Organizing Theory and the Current State of Flux

Von Bertalanffy described the concept of self-organizing systems as the process through which biological and social systems spontaneously transform to more complex forms when they no longer are able to incorporate the multiple and contradictory inputs from units both within and outside the system (1969). The point at which the system no longer can adjust within its current structure is a bifurcation point.

Prior to the bifurcation point, change is incremental and fairly predictable; there is a demand (outcomes assessment) and that demand is either resisted ("we need to study the process further" or "you don't really understand the purpose of higher education") or addressed ("we will institute post-graduate testing to assess learning"). At the bifurcation point, however, change becomes transformative and inherently unpredictable. This process is not unlike the assimilation-accommodation process in individual development. It appears that higher education well may be reaching a bifurcation point—that point in time at which the current structures no longer can accommodate the conflicting and contradictory demands that exist (Kennedy 1995). It is impossible to say whether this is actually the case because bifurcation points are only able to be identified retrospectively.

Given the accelerating demands on higher education in this country and the changing sociopolitical context in which it exists, higher education may have reached a point at which planned, orderly change that maintains current structures and relationships becomes nearly impossible. More specifically to the point of this report, we wonder what it will take for colleges and universities—and especially large doctoral and research universities—to better utilize the links among students' intellectual, social, and affective processes to enhance holistic learning. We address that question in this section.

In a time of great pressure—at a bifurcation point—systems enter a state of flux where boundaries are loosened, structures are relaxed, and resistance is eased. It is a time of great uncertainty because old rules and norms no longer apply. It also is a time of great opportunity in which the entire system is seeking a new, coherent, and more complex structure through which to accommodate the pressures it is experiencing. In this time, leadership and vision become that much more vital. According to self-organizing theory, social systems are unlike biological systems in that they are open to conscious, intentional human action. Therefore, outcomes of the transformation process may be unpredictable, but they still are open to human influence. Another aspect of self-organizing change is that the seeds of future states already exist in the current context. Which seeds may sprout is difficult to predict but also is open to potential influence.

One underlying assumption of this report is that colleges and universities are struggling to find ways to better meet the educational needs of their students. Another assumption is that they are attempting to make changes within the current cultural system that exists in higher education.

Operationalizing this latter assumption may not be possible. On a variety of levels the culture of the academy will need to be transformed. It is our assertion that to continue to enhance student learning in higher education, barriers and resistance need to be overcome both at an individual and an institutional level. If higher education is entering (or already is in) a period of flux, then transformational and visionary leadership can catalyze the changes that need to occur for holistic student learning to become dominant within higher education. It also is our argument that there exist within higher-education practices that could become widespread. To that end, in this section we focus on the organizational and institutional strategies and actions that could contribute to the proliferation of an integrated notion of student learning. This section presents strategies drawn from a synthesis of the research that has been conducted and the programs that have been implemented to best enhance the links among students' intellectual, social, and emotional development.

One underlying assumption of this report is that colleges and universities are struggling to find ways to better meet the educational needs of their students.

In-class vs. out-of-class dichotomy

As presented earlier, the current paradigm that exists in the literature (and especially the student affairs literature) encourages bridges to be built between faculty and student affairs professionals, between in-class and out-of-class experiences, and between academic affairs and student affairs. That is, the dichotomy between students' in-class (intellectual) and out-of-class (social and affective) experiences and promoting the link between them outside the classroom represents a theme in the literature regarding facilitating holistic learning (Miller and Jones 1981). For example, Smith expressed concern that by maintaining a distinction between classroom learning and life experience, colleges and universities are limiting the opportunities for students to become truly engaged in their learning (1988). Actions addressing this dichotomy will assist in the transformation of higher education and should be encouraged and rewarded. As discussed earlier, we see this particular focus on bridging as important, but limited.

If higher-education personnel undergo personal transformations as described in the previous section and if the strategies and actions that are described below are implemented, the traditional types of bridges will be incorporated into the overall transformation of student learning on campus. The intellectual, social, and emotional elements of learning can be integrated in and out of the classroom. Faculty can integrate intellectual, social, and emotional elements in the classroom, and student affairs professionals can do the same outside the classroom. One advantage to a focus on integrated out-of-class learning is the wide variety of learning that can be facilitated by those who work with students outside the classroom. As one chief student affairs officer indicated, "Because we are not bound by the curriculum, student affairs personnel have a more diverse palate with which to work than the faculty, who have to cover a particular content. What we can do that nobody else can is build informal opportunities for learning" (cited in Gamson 1991, p. 47).

Students' out-of-class lives contain a rich array of experiences that most clearly involve the social and affective dimensions of development. Out of class, students may interact with a diverse group of peers and other institutional agents (faculty, student affairs professionals, administrators); join clubs, teams, and other organizations, enter relationships, seek counseling and advice, work, socialize, travel, recreate, experience a wide range of positive and negative emotions and manage them; attend programs, symposia, and cultural events; and serve in leadership and paraprofessional positions. In addition, there are a host of out-of-class practices that potentially could integrate social, affective, and cognitive aspects of learning. These include living-learning centers, faculty-student out-of-class interaction, faculty-in-residence programs, new student orientation, leadership training and experience, learning assistance programs, service learning, the campus judicial/discipline process, and academic advising.

The past several decades have seen a dramatic increase in the recognition of the influence of the out-of-class experiences on students' persistence, success, satisfaction, and learning (Astin 1977, 1993; Boyer 1987; Chickering 1969; Chickering and Reisser 1993; Miller and Jones 1981). However, Kuh noted that students more frequently associated the intellectual and cognitive tasks of knowledge acquisition and academic-skills development with their experiences in the classroom, laboratory, and studios than they did with out-of-class experiences (1993b). For a more in-depth exploration of out-of-class learning we recommend *Student Learning Outside the Classroom: Transcending Artificial Boundaries* by Kuh, Douglas, Lund, and Ramin-Gyurnek. (1994). In this section we highlight the aspects of the research and literature that incorporate the relationships among intellectual, social, and emotional elements of learning and transcend traditional emphases on bridging in-class and out-of-class experiences. Implications for institutions moving toward developing an ethos of holistic learning include providing visionary, persistent, and pervasive leadership, promoting student involvement in their learning, developing learning communities, enhancing the educational climate of residence halls, and intentionally influencing the socialization of faculty and student affairs professionals.

Provide Visionary, Persistent, and Pervasive Leadership

That institutions of higher education are resistant to the types of changes needed to more effectively address student learning from a holistic perspective comes as no surprise to anyone who has worked in an institution of higher education. Many reform and transformation efforts have failed (Grant and Riesman 1978). Others initially have succeeded only to revert to more familiar forms. Of those that have succeeded and endured, one common element has been visionary, persistent, and pervasive leadership (Kuh 1993a; Roueche and Baker 1987; Schein 1985). Overcoming resistance and creating new cultural forms first requires a vision of that possible future state. Part of stating a vision must be the bringing to a conscious level the underlying culture that needs to change—a description of the outmoded assumptions, beliefs, values, and expectations. This becomes possible in times of cultural flux, which higher education may be experiencing now. For reform efforts to take hold, new directions, assumptions, beliefs, values, and expectations must be offered in place of the old.

Persistent leadership is required for several reasons. Foremost is that cultures themselves are quite persistent (Kuh 1993a; Schein 1985). Actions and behaviors may change, programs may be implemented, or institutional structures may be reorganized, and in the short run it may appear that change is occurring. However, without addressing and changing the underlying belief systems that supported previous structures, the new way of doing things eventually will come to look and feel like the old way. Culture change requires that energy continually be infused into the organizational system to maintain the changes being attempted. This is how external pressures are facilitators of change. By keeping constant pressure on a situation, energy remains focused in that area. Leaders can help focus the external pressures on the cultural change strategies.

Pervasive leadership implies both that the leadership of the institution must be seen as pervading the institution and that multiple leaders (both formal and informal) supporting and pushing the transformation must come from all segments and from throughout the hierarchy of the institution. Gone are the days of the all-powerful college president who could autocratically restructure an institution. Transformational change requires cultural leaders at most levels of the institution and in all sectors (academics, student affairs, students, alumni, administration). This also requires networks of communication and community among those pushing for change. One step in Total Quality Management's strategy for improving organizational processes is to bring people together in cross-functional teams—people from various areas of the organization, all of whom have some relationship to the process in question. An analog to this process could be created among people leading efforts to integrate the elements of student learning.

Promote Involvement

Student involvement has been a topic of focus for more than a decade (Astin 1984, 1985; Ory and Braskamp 1988; Smith 1988; The Study Group 1984). Kuh et al. conducted a study of 14 institutions noted for involving students in their education outside the classroom and recognizing the influence of out-of-class involvement on student learning (1991). Their work has provided a rich—and often cited—body of data. The involving colleges studied by Kuh et al. are most noted for their attention to the connections between the academic and social experiences of students. They found that by creating connections between the intellectual and the social and encouraging students to do the same, these institutions avoid putting students in the position of having to choose one over the other. Instead, students' academic and social—and emotional—experiences can be mutually reinforcing.

Miami University (Ohio) is one such institution which makes its commitment to integrating in-class and out-of-class learning experiences explicit:

*From its inception, Miami's mission emphasized stu-
dent learning from out-of-class experiences. The first
president of the university stated in unequivocal terms
the importance of the total learning experience and the
need for students to become involved in teaching other
students. . . . In the words of one Miami student,
"Student activities encourage us to use what we learn
in class—to integrate what's in class with real experience"* (Kuh et al. 1991, p. 53).

Kuh (1993b) reports on 14 types of outcomes mentioned by
the students in the study, and in each area there was evidence
of positive effects related to high levels of involvement.

TABLE 2

TAXONOMY OF OUTCOMES REPORT BY SENIORS IN INVOLVING COLLEGES
1. Self-awareness
2. Autonomy and self-directedness
3. Confidence and self-worth
4. Altruism
5. Reflective thought
6. Social competence
7. Practical competence
8. Knowledge acquisition
9. Academic skills
10. Application of knowledge
11. Aesthetic appreciation
12. Vocational competence
13. Sense of purpose
14. Other (includes such concepts as movement from conservative to liberal attitudes or vice versa, change in physical features, growing apart from spouse)

These individual outcomes reflect intellectual (knowledge
acquisition, academic skills, application of knowledge), social
(social competence), and affective (self-awareness, confidence
and self-worth, sense of purpose) elements. Kuh also noted
that the relationships among these outcomes were complex,
cumulative, and mutually shaping which emphasizes the
important contribution of the parts (intellectual, social, and
emotional) to the development of a greater whole (1993b).

Enhancing Student Learning

Methods to promote involvement include expanding the number of leadership roles on campus, developing and promoting activities and positions of responsibility, creating environments and situations in which all students have opportunities to participate and contribute, actively recruiting students into activities, fostering and rewarding student-initiated opportunities, and providing formal and informal awards for involvement (Kuh et al. 1991). A common element to these strategies is a significant degree of intentionality on the part of higher-education professionals to get students involved. Strategies can be carried out by faculty and student affairs professionals. Both can recruit students for leadership opportunities, activities, or honor societies and can nominate students for awards. And in no way is the concept of involvement restricted to cocurricular activities. The development of learning communities, for example, tends to focus more on curricular involvement.

Develop Learning Communities

Faculty who teach using a collaborative learning philosophy may be creating learning communities within their classrooms. However, learning communities typically are characterized by groups of students who take two or more classes together (Gabelnick et al. 1990). We further expand this definition to include programs that incorporate learning activities with living arrangements, most specifically exhibited in living-learning centers (Schroeder and Hurst 1996). Professors who teach the linked courses of the more typical academic learning community are expected to integrate the course content, materials, and if possible the assignments, so a broader understanding of each course is possible.

Academic learning communities may consist of linked pairs of classes, where the classes are composed only of students in the community, or they may consist of clusters of courses linked by an integrating seminar. At some institutions the integrating seminar is an orientation course (if the community is composed of first-year students); at other institutions the integrating seminar alternately is led by professors and academic advisors. Some learning communities are wide-scale collaborative learning strategies (sometimes called federated learning communities or coordinated studies programs) that permeate the entire curriculum—large groups of students register for a group of courses which are team-taught by two or three professors.

The most highly integrated model of learning community is the coordinated studies program (Gabelnick et al. 1990; Russo 1995; Tinto, Russo, and Kadel 1994). Coordinated studies programs (CSPs) typically are team-taught by two to four professors and are composed of three or four courses that relate in complementary ways to the CSP's central theme. For example, one CSP at Seattle Central Community College is called "Our Ways of Knowing: The African-American Experience and Social Change" and comprises courses in sociology, art, political science, and English. Students and all the faculty members meet for 11 to 18 hours each week in blocks of four to six hours. Meeting for large blocks of time gives the professors exceptional flexibility in scheduling and structuring tasks and assignments: Student presentations can be made, large group discussions can be held, movies can be viewed and discussed in one sitting, groups can be broken out for smaller seminar sections. "The key [characteristics of CSPs] of cross-disciplinary topics, team-teaching, continuous class meeting times, and regular small group activities creates a collaborative learning program that provides students with a distinctly different learning experience" (Tinto, Russo, and Kadel 1994).

While the most widely known federated learning community was established at the State University of New York at Stony Brook in 1977 (Romer 1985), a recent listing of established learning communities numbers at least 140 at colleges and universities throughout the United States (*Learning Communities Directory 1995*). This does not include the large number of professors at colleges and universities who are using collaborative learning strategies to develop learning communities in their individual classrooms, especially in writing courses (Bruffee 1987). The growth of learning communities reflects some progress in the movement toward integrating intellectual, social, and affective elements of learning. However, it falls far short of the recommendations of the Study Group on the Conditions of Excellence in American Higher Education (1984) that indicated "faculty should make greater use of active modes of teaching and require that students take greater responsibility for their learning" (p. 27) and recommended that "*every* institution of higher education should strive to create learning communities, organized around specific intellectual themes or tasks" (p. 33, emphasis added).

Nevertheless, learning communities are becoming institutionalized at many colleges and universities, and professional networks to support their use and development have been established. For example, The Washington Center for Improving the Quality of Undergraduate Education is a statewide consortium of 43 colleges and universities in Washington State which focuses on educational restructuring through learning communities, collaborative learning, faculty development, and cultural pluralism. The CUE (Collaboration in Undergraduate Education) Network is a subgroup of the American Association for Higher Education (AAHE). It sponsors programs at the annual meeting of AAHE and at other meetings to promote the use of collaborative learning strategies and publishes various papers and newsletters.

A final implication of learning communities, especially the highly thematically linked, team-taught strategies such as federated learning communities and coordinated studies programs, is that they spur students' higher order thinking skills (MacGregor 1991). Students in coordinated studies programs at The Evergreen State College and at several community colleges in Washington "generally made significant and unusual leaps in intellectual development during their learning community experience. Students . . . exited as early 'Multiplists,' significantly more advanced than their counterparts in control groups" (MacGregor 1991, p. 7).

In the next sections, we examine freshman interest groups (classroom-based learning community) and living-learning centers (residence-based learning community). We focus on these because of the many opportunities both offer for cooperation and collaboration among faculty, student affairs professionals, and students.

Freshman interest groups
Freshman interest groups, or FIGs, are groups of 20 to 25 students enrolled in two or three common courses (Gabelnick, MacGregor, Matthews, and Smith 1990; Goodsell 1993). The courses that make up a FIG are chosen to reflect a general theme and frequently include some type of composition or writing course. For example, a FIG at the University of Washington called "Speech and Drama" was

composed of "Introduction to the Theater," "Oral Interpretation of Literature," and "Composition"; a FIG called "The Ancient World" was composed of "Survey of Ancient Western Art," "The Ancient World" (an introductory history course), and "Humanities Writing." Not all of the courses are composed solely of students in the FIG. One or two of the courses may be large lecture courses in which the FIG students make up a small portion of the class. Typically, however, the FIG students meet in their own section of a composition course. This especially helps to break down the anonymity that is prevalent in large lecture classes.

In addition to the three courses, the students meet once a week in a separate seminar led by an upperclass peer advisor. In these FIG seminars students may discuss the subject matter of one or more of the classes or university life in general. Some FIG programs expect students to attend one social or cultural event together, such as seeing a play on campus or going as a group to a museum. The peer advisors are supervised weekly by an administrator who may be an academic advisor, an assistant dean of a college, or some related person. Because much of the social networking between students happens on their own or through the encouragement of the peer advisor, faculty members may be asked to do very little for the FIG. For this very reason FIGs have been implemented at large universities where the faculty culture tends to be quite resistant to change, where faculty reward systems are strongly focused on research and scholarship, and where large lecture classes are the norm.

It bears repeating that one of the most beneficial aspects of collaborative learning strategies for students is the opportunity to meet their social needs such as making friends, learning their way around and fitting into a large campus, and sharing coping strategies while at the same time focusing on their intellectual development. One student in a freshman interest group reported, "One of the biggest reasons for joining a FIG group was to meet people. The way the university is set up it is practically impossible to meet people unless you subdivide it into smaller groups" (Tinto and Goodsell 1993, p. 15). Although the need to find one's way around a campus may be met during a student's first semester, other benefits of social interaction continue into subsequent semesters. The social network of peers that is established through learning communities allows other academic-support mechanisms to operate. As implied above, the comfort that students report as a result of knowing a core group of peers has implications for counteracting the anonymity of large lecture classes.

Learning communities may or may not require students to meet in study groups outside of class, but they provide peer pressure to attend classes, as this student related: "The reason why I go [to composition] usually is because that's a smaller class; if you're missing, everyone knows you're gone. And you kind of feel, that's the only class I really feel obligated, like I have to be there every day, so I show up to each class" (Tinto and Goodsell 1993, p. 19). Another student talked about classes in general: "[A] nice thing about FIGs is that since you know everyone, they really encourage you not to skip out. There's more encouragement not to miss classes. If you go to your first class, then there's everyone telling you to go to your second" (Tinto and Goodsell 1993, p. 19). Although these comments may not warm the hearts of faculty members who hope that students will attend their classes because of an overwhelming interest in the subject matter, they do reinforce the importance of peer dynamics in classes and the need to shape them to the best educational purposes possible.

The role of student affairs in classroom-based learning communities. The implementation of classroom-based learning communities (freshman interest groups and coordinated-studies programs, for example) involve many important administrative tasks for which faculty members may be unprepared or may be unwilling to address. Student affairs professionals such as senior student affairs officers, the registrar, academic advisors, and others can play instrumental roles in implementing these types of learning strategies. Senior student affairs officers can initiate, or support the initiation of, academic learning communities, depending upon what units of the university report to them. As indicated above, committed leadership is one key to the successful implementation of change in any college or university. By educating other student affairs professionals about learning communities and by supporting efforts to establish them, senior student affairs officers can have a significant influence on the learning climate of an institution. Senior student affairs officers also can:

■ 1. Assign an individual to administer the learning community program.

Many institutions that have some type of classroom-based learning community also assign an individual to administer the program. This person might operate out of the provost's office or the dean of students' office or may be a professor given release time to act as a faculty fellow. Often, he or she is experienced both in academic and student affairs. Such an administrator's responsibilities typically include selecting appropriate courses and times for the target population of each community, ensuring enrollment, providing faculty and/or peer advisor training, and conducting evaluation of the program.

■ 2. Solicit input from academic advisors early in the development of the program.

Academic advisors are unsung heroes and heroines on many campuses, and they play three major roles in the development and implementation of academic learning communities. Academic advisors are in the best position to know what courses should be grouped together to serve the needs of students, and they know what courses students typically take. This becomes essential when it is time to register students in a community. Registration is not the time to find out that advisors will not advise students into a learning community composed of geology, music, and composition if a student has a weak placement score in science. Advisors also are well-versed in the complex topic of prerequisite courses; learning communities that include prerequisites to major course requirements may appeal to students more than those composed of electives.

Not only must academic advisors be involved in course selection and community composition, they also play a vital role in recruiting and registering students into learning communities.

Not only must academic advisors be involved in course selection and community composition, they also play a vital role in recruiting and registering students into learning communities. For communities designed for first-year students, for example, advisors may be the only professional on campus whom students consult when selecting courses. As students complete a semester and begin to network with their peers and talk to faculty regarding course selection, learning communities may be recommended by these other people, but first-year students usually rely on the recommendations of advisors.

Academic advisors can be involved a third way, depend-

---

ing upon the structure of the learning community. As described previously, some communities contain an integrating seminar or orientation course. These may be taught by faculty members or advisors or both, depending upon the intent of the seminar. Even in freshman interest group meetings led by peer advisors, professional academic advisors often are invited to attend a session or two to discuss choices of majors and future course registration or for career exploration. Two of the benefits of academic advisors and faculty members working together to teach seminars are a sharing of information and skills and an appreciation for each other's work. Advisors may become more knowledgeable about a professor's style or approach to teaching, and professors may gain trust in being able to refer to an advisor a student in need of assistance.

■ 3. Include the registrar in learning community planning.

The registrar is another student affairs professional who is important in the planning and development of learning communities. In addition to ensuring that courses are identified appropriately in the schedule of courses (if they are restricted to a certain community, for example), the registrar can devise ways to link courses so that students who are supposed to take sections together actually do so. The best-integrated course assignments will come to naught if the students do not end up in the same classes. Given the months of time in advance that schedules are planned, if this seemingly simple aspect of learning community implementation waits until the last minute, the implementation itself will not work.

■ 4. Have student affairs professionals train peer advisors.

Finally, at institutions that seek to develop FIGs in particular, the training of upperclass peer advisors may be modeled after training programs for residence hall advisors or other types of peer educators. Student affairs professionals work closely with students who are involved on campus and therefore may be excellent resources for identifying students who can become peer advisors. In addition, the coordinating administrator of a freshman interest group program could work closely with the student-activities office or the

student programming board so as to alert FIG peer advisors
of upcoming events that the FIGs might attend. In these
ways and others that emerge as learning communities grow,
student affairs professionals can contribute significantly to
the integrated learning environment that collaborative strategies provide.

Living-learning centers

Another form of learning community, living-learning centers
are a step beyond traditional residence halls, in that faculty,
offices, and classrooms are integrated into the residence unit
(Pascarella, Terenzini, and Blimling 1994). Living-learning
centers may not always meet the traditional definition of a
learning community in that students may not take classes
together. Instead, the linking that takes place is through the
social element of the living space. Smith and Raney, in *The
North American Directory of Residential Colleges and Living
Learning Centers,* identified 64 institutions that have such
programs and about half of them had developed their programs during the previous 10 years (1993). Ryan identified
six emphases of typical living-learning center programs:
ethics, citizenship, community, instruction, cocurricular programming, and peer learning (1995). These particular
emphases reflect the intellectual, social, and emotional elements of student learning.

Living-learning centers have been shown to enhance students' academic performance through integration of intellectual and social elements of learning (Pascarella and Terenzini
1980, 1981). This includes significantly greater informal interaction with faculty and a stronger intellectual focus within
the living community. One exceptional example of an integrated living-learning program is that of the University at
Stony Brook (Stein 1995). This campus has five living-learning centers with the diverse themes of Human Sexual and
Gender Development, Science and Engineering, International
Studies, Wellness, and Environmental Studies. Two new centers being developed are Health and Society and The Arts.

Stony Brook's department of residence programs also has
an Honors College and WISE, a residential program for
women in science and engineering. In addition to the typical
social and recreational amenities, each of these residence
units has classrooms, faculty offices, study areas, a multi-
media room, and a computer room. Each program is staffed

with a faculty director and a full-time residence hall director. All provide special seminars, courses, and programs related to the topic area and depending upon the program some centers have academic minors available in the topic area, topic-related internships, cultural activities, and integrated cocurricular activities. During the 1994-95 academic year 51 credit-bearing courses were offered in the residence halls involving 850 students and generating almost 1,400 credit hours. Many of the courses were cofacilated by faculty and student affairs professionals. This program represents a significant commitment to linking faculty and student affairs and bringing the classroom to the out-of-class world.

Multiple and overlapping learning communities
Earlier, we pointed out that by holding an image of a single, ideal college community we might be blinding ourselves to the possibilities that exist for creating multiple subcommunities on our campuses. The power of learning communities is that they provide the time and the place(s) for students, faculty, and student affairs professionals to meet and develop subcommunities that revolve around the subject matter of the linked courses or bring an academic focus to a living environment.

FIGs usually do not require students to meet together outside of class, but because students have the same schedules and the same courses the likelihood that they will get together is dramatically increased. The interdisciplinary nature of most living-learning centers and freshman interest groups encourages faculty members to communicate with others outside of their academic department, and it gives them a reason to do so. "Collaborative teaching is a departure from such traditional methods of faculty development as sabbaticals and extra research time, which . . . isolate professors rather than bring them together to trade pedagogical ideas" (Monaghan 1989, p. A13). Institutions that implement learning communities benefit in many ways—they allow subcommunities of students, faculty, and student affairs professionals to form, which in turn provides peer support for students and professional development for faculty and student affairs professionals.

By providing opportunities for student, faculty, and student affairs subcommunities to form, institutions also create the opportunity for change in those subcommunities. Rather than delegating the curricular change process to a committee and expecting a standardized answer to apply to the entire institution, institutions would do well to turn over the process to small groups of students and faculty who can create collaborative structures to fit their particular purposes, whether it is meeting the needs of first-year students, commuters, students taking developmental level courses, or honors students.

> *We need to give serious attention to the argument that the attainment of the goals of enhanced student involvement and achievement is possible only when institutions alter the settings in which students are asked to learn. Rather than focus on student behaviors and student obligations alone, we should more carefully consider the character of our own obligations to construct the sorts of educational settings in which students—all students, not just some—will want to become involved* (Tinto et al. 1993, p. 21).

Providing the structure and the space for multiple, overlapping learning communities is an important way for institutions to allow for the creation of multiple, interdisciplinary subcommunities. Another important institutional consideration are the faculty reward and support systems. To encourage proliferation of learning communities as well as encourage the use of alternative pedagogies and collaborative learning strategies, institutions must restructure the faculty-reward structure—and their associated assessment systems— to support collaborative and cross-disciplinary work.

Enhance the Educational Climate of Residence Halls
As evidenced by the research on living-learning centers, living in residence halls has been noted as having great potential to enhance student learning and development (e.g., Astin 1977, 1993; Chickering 1974). However, the emphasis here is on the word "potential." For while Pascarella, Terenzini, and Blimling found in their review of the literature that living on campus, as opposed to commuting, significantly enhanced student involvement, satisfaction, and persistence to graduation, the evidence was less clear on other aspects of learning and development (1994).

For example, Pascarella et al. found that the impact of

residential living on personal growth and development, and development related to values, attitudes, and moral judgment was mixed, though still tended to be positive (1994). Overall, Pascarella and Terenzini found that living on campus "tends to promote somewhat greater increases in personal autonomy and independence, intellectual disposition, and the development of mature interpersonal relationships" (1991, p. 262). In a meta-analysis of research that specifically addressed the academic impact of living in residence halls, however, Blimling (1989) found no advantage to living in the residence halls for academic achievement and, in fact, suggested that "the normative social milieu of residence halls can at times provide greater opportunities for socializing than for studying" (Pascarella et al., 1994, p. 30).

Pascarella et al. identified what they called a "major causal mechanism" related to enhanced outcomes for residence students. This was that living on campus enhanced the amount of social interaction students had with faculty and peers. "Place of residence exerted its major educational impact by shaping the nature of student's social/interpersonal environment" (1994, p. 28). Thus, when considering the influence of living-learning centers and Blimling's findings about traditional residence halls, the social nature of students' experience can either enhance the intellectual achievement of students or detract from it.

The implication is that conscious and deliberate actions must be taken to integrate intellectual, social, and affective elements of student learning in the residence halls. Chickering and Reisser noted that staff members can maximize the intellectual, social, and emotional developmental influence of residence-hall living by:

1. Incorporating learning activities into living units;
2. Adapting existing halls to allow a balance of interaction and privacy and to permit a more personalized environment;
3. Enhancing community by building new units that are small enough to allow maximum participation but large enough to allow more experienced students to induct newer ones into the culture;
4. Improving both the "fit" and the diversity by placing students carefully; and
5. Using regulations, policies, and hall-management

strategies as tools for fostering autonomy, interdependence, and integrity (1993, p. 402).

Certainly residence halls offer a wonderful potential opportunity to enhance out-of-class holistic learning, but today relatively few students have the luxury of living on campus, no less in a living-learning center. This is due, in part, to the rising cost of college attendance and living on campus, the increase in part-time students, and the increase in returning adult students, many of whom prefer living arrangements other than residence halls. What follows are additional methods and activities for enhancing holistic student learning.

Intentionally Influence Faculty and Student Affairs Socialization

In addition to aligning and changing organizational structures and forms, institutions must pay great attention to the cultural socialization and orientation of its members—specifically faculty and student affairs professionals. Faculty and student affairs professionals arrive on campus with assumptions, beliefs, experiences, and expectations of each other already in place. This cultural learning has taken place over time as undergraduates and graduate students and as professionals at other institutions.

Related to our arguments in the previous section—that for holistic learning to be a focus in our institutions individuals will need to change—we suggest that institutions can influence that process through an intentional focus on faculty and student affairs socialization. Three ways in which this can be accomplished are implementing teaching assistant training programs, incorporating an emphasis on student learning in student affairs graduate preparation programs, and implementing professional staff orientation and ongoing training.

1. Implement teaching assistant training programs.

Today's faculty have been socialized into the current cultural system. Not only are they committed to the current expectations and reward systems, but to a large degree they have self-selected into an academic career because of the tasks primarily associated with the job (i.e., research, scholarship, and writing). A first step toward transforming faculty culture is to examine the entry point of the academic pipeline and influence the types of individuals pursuing such a career (Kennedy 1995; Tierney and Rhoads 1994).

Merton has labeled the part of the socialization process that workers experience prior to entry into an organization as anticipatory socialization (1963). One aspect of anticipatory socialization is that prior to entry into an organization, profession, or other cultural unit individuals determine whether there is sufficient degree of fit between their values, assumptions, and expectations and those they perceive as important in the cultural unit (Van Maanen 1976, 1984). It used to be that people chose to become college professors because they wanted to teach and conduct research or other scholarship. Today most people enter the profession—especially at research universities—because their primary interests are to conduct research or pursue other scholarship (Bowen and Schuster 1986). If they want to teach, it is of secondary importance and likely to diminish in importance as they proceed through their culture of orientation—their doctoral program (Van Maanen 1976, 1984).

Therefore, doctoral programs must play a significant role in changing the current faculty culture. Recently, teaching assistant, or TA, training programs have been developed and are spreading (Lawrenz 1992; Nyquist 1989; Poole 1991). TA training programs that focus on holistic student learning can do a number of things. They can train potential faculty members in the skills of teaching, breaking the cycle of ineffective, didactic, lecture style teaching that many college teachers use because it was what they were exposed to as college students. TA training programs, by their very existence, can put into action the importance of teaching. Not only will the importance of teaching be espoused, it will be enacted. It is through these activities that culture can be influenced.

We recommend that these programs be enhanced and disseminated among all doctoral and research institutions. Care needs to be taken in who is selected to facilitate these programs in that training should go beyond traditional pedagogies and incorporate aspects of liberation and constructivist pedagogies. These emergent teaching philosophies have been shown to actively make use of the social and affective dimensions of students' experience in the classroom. Additionally, if faculty adopt these alternative pedagogies, they will need to be prepared to deal with student

emotions in the classroom, especially negative and potentially toxic emotions of anger, frustration, grief, hostility, sad-
ness, and depression. This is an issue about which didactic
lecturers rarely need to be concerned. TA training programs
should not train faculty to be counselors but should include
practice in experiencing the discomfort of students express-
ing emotions, how to incorporate emotions into the learning
experience, training in active listening skills, and training in
referral skills and sources.

**2. Review student affairs graduate preparation
programs.** Student affairs preparation programs traditionally
have incorporated coursework focused on understanding
and applying student development theory. Included in these
theories have been the work of cognitive development theorists, especially Perry (1970), Belenky et al. (1986), King and
Kitchener (1994), and Baxter Magolda (1992). As indicated
previously, the student affairs field also is involved in a discussion about its role in student learning. This discussion, in
the form of journals, conferences, and Internet listservs, is
healthy and necessary. It also needs to incorporate consideration of the role that graduate preparation programs play in
the perpetuation of the current cultural assumptions about
faculty (they are unconcerned about students and student
affairs professionals, they are stuck in the classroom, and
they only care about research and scholarship), about learning and development (the tendency to focus only on social
and affective dimensions), about where learning takes place
(academic learning takes place in the classroom; social and
affective development take place outside the classroom),
and about how the situation needs to be addressed (bring
faculty out of the classroom, bridge in- and out-of-class
experiences, and link academic and student affairs).

Specific recommendations for student affairs graduate
preparation programs to consider are:
a. Include liberation theory, constructivist pedagogy, and
   collaborative learning in the curriculum. These concepts,
   theories, and philosophies can be incorporated into introductory courses as well as into developmental and
   administrative courses.
b. Teach from a critical cultural perspective and encourage
   students to focus these critical skills on their own development and on the culture of the field of student affairs.

Teaching about the topics of liberation theory, constructivist pedagogy, and collaborative learning are not enough. Faculty in preparation programs need to exhibit these philosophies in their own practice. This includes teaching from a critical cultural perspective and expecting students to practice these skills as well.

c. Incorporate learning theory into the curriculum. With the focus on student learning in the field of student affairs, additional resources on student learning are emerging (King 1996; Stage 1996, for example) and can be incorporated into such courses as student development theory.

d. Incorporate the expectation of adopting a holistic learning perspective in internship and assistantship experiences. Internship and assistantship experiences are where emerging student affairs professionals gain valuable experience and skills but also where the current culture of the field is reinforced. These experiences can serve as the laboratories in which graduate students can critically analyze the culture of student affairs departments and other student affairs contexts; practice integrating intellectual, social, and emotional elements of student learning; and discuss their experiences with other students and faculty.

3. Offer support and training for faculty and student affairs. Time, support, and training are the most important resources an institution can provide to faculty and student affairs professionals who are attempting to enhance or transform their philosophy of professional practice. Faculty need to be supported by the institution in their use of collaborative learning.

At some institutions this takes the form of being given release time during a semester previous to the implementation of collaborative learning so that comprehensive planning can occur. This is especially crucial for faculty who will be team-teaching and need to coordinate their efforts with others, but it also is true for individual faculty as well. Support can be given in the form of faculty-development seminars where faculty members can meet to discuss issues related to implementation. This can involve case studies, trying out a strategy that later will be used in a class, or problem-solving about an actual class. Some institutions pay faculty a stipend for the extra time they will spend. Even at institutions in which collaborative learning is firmly in place, faculty tend to rotate into and out of participation, especially with those strategies that are more intensive such as learning communities and coordinated studies programs.

We also recommend that four-year institutions adopt a strategy similar to that of several community colleges which require all new faculty to take a set number of classes or workshops in student learning and experience (for example, teaching strategies, cognitive development, student socialization, pedagogy, student assessment, learning styles) after they are hired. This will require significant institutional commitment and support, especially given the traditional faculty value of autonomy. Institutional reward systems must be structured to require or encourage them to participate.

We recommend going beyond faculty and requiring the same of student affairs professionals. This sends a message to faculty about the importance the institution places on teaching and student learning and a message to student affairs professionals about the need to incorporate student learning into their work in the affective and social realms. An additional benefit is that it places new student affairs professionals and new faculty together in a milieu where they are working together, learning together, and learning about each other and each other's culture. Physical proximity and the resultant communication have been shown as effective in bridging cultural gaps (Love 1990).

Ongoing faculty training also is recommended. If, as suggested, the faculty role is partitioned, faculty whose primary task is to teach could be encouraged to become master teachers through ongoing training and development. Additional coursework, mentoring, apprenticing to a master teacher, and supervised practice could be required as part of the promotion and tenure process. However, everyone who teaches at a college or university should be required to continue to hone their skills as instructors.

Summary
Higher education has struggled for a long time under the strain of increasing fragmentation: fragmentation of the learning process, fragmentation of disciplines and knowledge, fragmentation of the administrative structure, and fragmentation of community. A long history and strong cultural forces have acted as barriers to efforts at reforming and transforming higher education. But now forces both from

within and without have gathered that are exerting tremendous pressure on the entire enterprise. These forces may be loosening the barriers to integrating the intellectual, social, and emotional elements of learning. By experimenting with alternative pedagogies, developing learning communities, enhancing the learning that occurs outside the classroom, adopting a critical cultural perspective, and expanding the notion of learning, institutions, faculty, and student affairs professionals may be able foster this transformation and enhance holistic student learning.

SUMMARY

You can lead me to college but you can't make me think.

—T-shirt printed at Duke University in response to the recommendations of the University's Task Force on the Intellectual Climate.

A story in the *Chronicle of Higher Education* described the changes faculty and administrators at Duke University have initiated in an attempt to promote the intellectual life of the campus (Gose, March 8, 1996). Actions included housing first-year students in a cluster of residence halls with faculty members in residence, deferring Greek rush from the fall to the spring semester of the first year, moving fraternities out of some of the best campus housing, banning keg parties on campus, and starting a new program that "encourages professors and students to get together socially for activities like hiking or watching a play" (Gose 1996, p. A33).

The long-term effects of the initiatives, begun in fall 1995, will take some time to unfold, but we see in them many of the concepts highlighted in this report—persistent leadership from the president and faculty, a recognition that intellectual development can be fostered outside the classroom, and some head-on attempts to change elements of the student culture by changing residence and social policies. What were not described were any changes in the ways that social and emotional processes are addressed in classes: Does the predominant mode of instruction take place in a large lecture hall with little opportunity for student input and interaction? Are students being asked about the changing campus culture in their courses? The story of cultural change at Duke may be an important one, with lessons to assist other institutions with their efforts at reform.

Based on the research cited in this report, it should be evident that higher education must move in the direction of holistic student learning. At the beginning we acknowledged the multiple pressures on higher education that may be serving as catalysts for reform—a shift in paradigms from positivistic toward naturalistic, qualitative methods of inquiry; the emergence of new disciplines that cross traditional disciplinary boundaries; calls for reform from within higher education during the past decade; and external pressures such as governmental calls for outcomes assessment and institu-

Based on the research cited in this report, it should be evident that higher education must move in the direction of holistic student learning.

tional accountability. These last factors—assessment and accountability—need to be addressed as a part of all the strategies we have suggested for integrating student learning. If reform efforts are to gain support, both internally and externally, additional research needs to be conducted in at least two areas: assessing holistic learning in and out of the classroom and assessing efforts such as Duke's that attempt to change and shape campus cultures to support the practice of holistic learning.

Furthermore, assessing holistic learning in and out of the classroom will require an expanded and transformed idea of assessment. If we keep looking for the same kinds of results in the same kinds of places with the same kinds of methods (such as test scores on standardized instruments), we will miss the results that an enhanced focus on holistic learning can produce. The phrase "if your only tool is a hammer, every problem looks like a nail" is applicable here. An enhanced focus on holistic learning across the campus can yield other results, such as strengthened critical thinking skills, increased ability to think across disciplines, a better appreciation for the role of social and emotional processes in learning, enhanced emotional intelligence, leadership skills, and additional abilities to work collaboratively (Goleman 1995).

Not only do we need to address issues of assessment and accountability by looking for different results, we need to use different methods. Assessing culture change requires sustained, detailed study—not a single administration of a survey. This is in line with the paradigmatic shift cited, but it needs to be intentionally integrated into assessment efforts. Faculty and staff trained in methods of positivistic inquiry naturally will look in toward the methods of positivistic inquiry (structured surveys and objective tests, for example) when called on to plan assessment efforts. Culture change need not start as campuswide initiatives. Starting with particular sites (such as classes, student organizations, and residence halls) or groups (students, faculty, and student affairs professionals, for example) and studying efforts involved will contribute to the knowledge base of change efforts focused on creating cultures supportive of holistic learning.

This report contains many ideas for addressing the integration of students' intellectual, social, and emotional development. Many other strategies exist and many have yet to be put into practice, but we hope that the variety of those listed will be sufficient to spark discussion and debate about the issues raised in this report—the detrimental nature of the divide between students' intellectual, social, and emotional development; the need to focus on more holistic practices of student learning; and the barriers to doing so presented by the cultures surrounding the roles of faculty and student affairs professionals.

REFERENCES

American College Personnel Association. 1994. *The Student Learning Imperative: Implications for Student Affairs.* Washington, D.C.: American College Personnel Association.

American Council on Education. 1937. *The Student Personnel Point of View.* Washington, D.C.: American Council on Education.

———. 1949. *The Student Personnel Point of View.* Washington, D.C.: American Council on Education.

Appleton, J.R., C. Briggs, and J. Rhatigan. 1978. *Pieces of Eight.* Portland, Ore.: National Association of Student Personnel Administrators.

Astin, A. 1977. *Four Critical Years.* San Francisco: Jossey-Bass.

———. 1984. Student Involvement: A Developmental Theory for Higher Education. *Journal of College Student Personnel* 25: 297-308.

———. 1985. *Achieving Educational Excellence: A Critical Assessment of Priorities and Practices in Higher Education.* San Francisco: Jossey-Bass.

———. 1993. *What Matters in College? Four Critical Years Revisited.* San Francisco: Jossey-Bass.

Attinasi, L.C. 1989. "Getting In: Mexican-Americans' Perceptions of University Attendance and the Implications for Freshman Year Persistence." *Journal of Higher Education* 60: 247-77.

Baldridge, J.V. 1981. "Nightmares vs. Visions: Structuring Stronger Partnerships for Institutional Vitality." *National ACAC Journal* 26(1): 13-21.

Barrow, J.C. 1986. *Fostering Cognitive Development.* San Francisco: Jossey-Bass.

Baxter Magolda, M.B. 1992. *Knowing and Reasoning in College: Gender-Related Patterns in Students' Intellectual Development.* San Francisco: Jossey-Bass.

———. 1995. "The Integration of Relational and Impersonal Knowing in Young Adults' Epistemological Development." *Journal of College Student Development* 36: 205-16.

Bean, J.P., and J.W. Creswell. 1980. "Student Attrition Among Women at Liberal Arts College." *Journal of College Student Personnel* 21: 320-27.

Becker, H.S., B. Geer, and E.C. Hughes. 1968. *Making the Grade: The Academic Side of College Life.* New York: Wiley.

Belenky, M.F., B.M. Clinchy, N.R. Goldberger, and J.M. Tarule. 1986. *Women's Ways of Knowing: The Development of Self, Mind, and Voice.* New York: Basic Books.

Bless, H., G. Bohner, N. Schwarz, and F. Stack. 1990. "Mood and Persuasion: A Cognitive Response Analysis." *Personality and*

Socialpsychology Bulletin 16: 331-45.

Blimling, G.S. 1989. "A Meta-Analysis of the Influence of College Residence Halls on Academic Performance." *Journal of College Student Development* 30: 298-308.

Blimling, G.S., and A.S. Alschuler. 1996. "Creating a Home for the Spirit of Learning: Contributions of Student Development Educators." *Journal of College Student Development* 37: 203-16.

Boekaerts, M. 1993. "Being Concerned With Well-Being and With Learning." *Educational Psychologist* 28(2): 149-67.

Bok, D. April 27, 1988. "Report to Harvard Board of Overseers." *Chronicle of Higher Education* 34: B4.

Bonwell, C.C., and J.A. Eison. 1991. *Active Learning: Creating Excitement in the Classroom.* ASHE-ERIC Higher Education Report No. 1. Washington, D.C.: Association for the Study of Higher Education. ED 336 049. 121 pp. MF-01; PC-05.

Bouton, C., and R.Y. Garth. 1983. *Learning in Groups.* New Directions for Teaching and Learning No. 14. San Francisco: Jossey-Bass.

Bowen, H.R. 1977. *Investment in Learning.* San Francisco: Jossey-Bass.

Bowen, H.R., and J.H. Schuster. 1986. *American Professors: A National Resource Imperiled.* New York: Oxford University Press.

Boyer, E.L. 1987. *College: The Undergraduate Experience in America.* New York: Harper & Row.

———. October 1, 1988. Address. *The University Record: 1.* Southeast Missouri State University.

———. 1990. *Scholarship Reconsidered: Priorities of the Professoriate.* Princeton, N.J.: Carnegie Foundation for the Advancement of Teaching. ED 326 149. 151 pp. MF-01; PC not available EDRS.

Brooks, J.G., and M.G. Brooks. 1993. *In Search of Understanding: The Case for Constructivist Classrooms.* Alexandria, Va.: Association for Supervision and Curriculum Development. ED 366 428. 143 pp. MF-01; PC not available EDRS.

Brophy, J. 1985. "Teacher-Student Interaction." In *Teacher Expectancies,* edited by J.B. Dusk. Hillside, N.J.: Erlbaum Associates.

Brown, R.D. 1972. *Student Development in Tomorrow's Higher Education: A Return to the Academy.* Washington, D.C.: American College Personnel Association.

Brown, S.S. 1990. "Strengthening Ties to Academic Affairs." In *New Futures for Students Affairs: Building a Vision for Professional Leadership and Practice,* edited by M.J. Barr and M.L. Upcraft.

San Francisco: Jossey-Bass.

Brubacher, J.S., and W. Rudy. 1976. *Higher Education in Transition: A History of American Colleges and Universities, 1636-1976.* New York: Harper & Row.

Bruffee, K. 1984. "Collaborative Learning and the Conversation of Mankind." *College English* 46: 635-52.

———. 1987. "The Art of Collaborative Learning: Making the Most of Knowledgeable Peers." *Change* 19(2): 42-47.

———. 1993. *Collaborative Learning: Higher Education, Interdependence, and the Authority of Knowledge.* Baltimore: The Johns Hopkins University Press.

Buerk, D. 1985. "The Voices of Women Making Meaning in Mathematics." *Journal of Education* 167: 59-70.

Cabello, B., and R.D. Terrell. 1994. "Making Students Feel Like Family: How Teachers Create Warm and Caring Classroom Climates." *Journal of Classroom Interaction* 29(1): 17-23.

Campus Life: In Search of Community. 1990. Princeton, N.J.: The Carnegie Foundation for the Advancement of Teaching. ED 320 492. 157 pp. MF-01; PC not available EDRS.

Caple, R.B. 1996. "The Learning Debate: A Historical Perspective." *Journal of College Student Development* 37: 193-202.

Chaffee, E.E., and W.G. Tierney. 1988. *College Culture and Leadership Strategies.* New York: American Council on Education and Macmillan.

Chickering, A.W. 1969. *Education and Identity.* San Francisco: Jossey-Bass.

———. 1974. *Commuting Versus Resident Students: Overcoming Education Inequities of Living Off Campus.* San Francisco: Jossey-Bass.

Chickering, A.W., and Z.F. Gamson. 1987. "Seven Principles for Good Practice in Undergraduate Education." *American Association of Higher Education Bulletin* 39(7): 3-7.

Chickering, A.W., and L. Reisser. 1993. *Education and Identity.* 2d ed. San Francisco: Jossey-Bass.

Connell, J.P. 1990. "Context, Self and Action: A Motivational Analysis of Self-System Processes Across the Lifespan." In *The Self in Transition: Infancy to Childhood,* edited by D. Cicchetti. Chicago: University of Chicago Press.

Cooper, J.L., and R. Mueck. 1990. "Student Involvement in Learning: Cooperative Learning and College Instruction." *Journal on Excellence in College Teaching* 1(1): 68-76.

Council of Student Personnel Associations in Higher Education. 1975. "Student Development Services in Post Secondary

Education." *Journal of College Student Personnel* 16: 524-28.

Crookston, B.B. 1974. "A Design for an Intentional Democratic Community." In *Student Development and Education in College Residence Halls* , edited by D.A. DeCoster and P. Mable. Washington, D.C.: American College Personnel Association.

Cross, K.P. 1976. *Accent on Learning.* San Francisco: Jossey-Bass.

Cross, K.P., and T.A. Angelo. 1992. *Classroom Assessment Techniques: A Handbook for Faculty.* San Francisco: Jossey-Bass.

Cuseo, J. 1991. "Potential Benefits for Cooperative Learning for Promoting Social and Emotional Development." *Cooperative Learning and College Teaching Newsletter* 1(2): 4-8. California State University at Dominguez Hills: Network for Cooperative Learning in Higher Education.

Davis, M.T., and C.C. Schroeder. 1983. "New Students in Liberal Arts Colleges: Threat or Challenge?" In *Pioneers and Pallbearers: Perspectives on Liberal Education,* edited by J. Watson and R. Stevens. Macon, Ga.: Mercer University Press.

DeVries, R., and L. Kohlberg. 1987. *Constructivist Early Education: Overview and Comparison With Other Programs.* Washington, D.C.: National Association for the Education of Young Children.

Easton, J.Q. 1983. "Chicago Colleges Identify Effective Teachers, Students." *Community and Junior College Journal* 54: 26-27.

Erickson, B.L., and D.W. Strommer. 1991. *Teaching College Freshmen.* San Francisco: Jossey-Bass.

Erikson, E. 1959. "Identity and the Life-Cycle. " *Psychological Issues Monograph* 1(1): 1-171.

Ewell, P.J. 1994. "A Preliminary Study of the Feasibility and Utility for National Policy of Instructional Good Practice Indicators in Undergraduate Education." U.S. Department of Education, Office of Educational Research and Improvement, Report NCES 94-437. Washington, D.C.: National Center for Education Statistics. ED 372 718. 68 pp. MF-01; PC-03.

Fassinger, P.A. 1995. "Understanding Classroom Interaction: Students and Professors Contributions to Students' Silence." *Journal of Higher Education* 66: 82-96.

Feldman, K., and T. Newcomb. 1969. *The Impact of College on Students.* San Francisco: Jossey-Bass.

Fenske, R.H. 1989. "Current Issues." In *Student Services: A Handbook for the Profession,* edited by U. Delworth and G.R. Hanson. San Francisco: Jossey-Bass.

Festinger, L. 1957. *A Theory of Cognitive Dissonance.* Palo Alto, Calif.: Stanford University Press.

Flores, B., P.T. Cousin, and E. Diaz. 1991. "Transforming Deficit

Myths About Learning, Language and Culture." *Language Arts* 68: 369-79.

Forrest, A. 1985. "Creating Conditions for Student and Institutional Success." In *Increasing Student Retention: Effective Programs and Practices for Reducing the Dropout Rate*, edited by L. Noel, R. Levitz, and D. Saluri. San Francisco: Jossey-Bass.

Fosnot, C.T. 1993. Preface. In *In Search of Understanding: The Case for Constructivist Classrooms*, by J.G. Brooks and M.G. Brooks. Alexandria, Va.: Association for Supervision and Curriculum Development. ED 366 428. 143 pp. MF-01; PC not available EDRS.

Freire, P. 1970. *Pedagogy of the Oppressed*. New York: Continuum.

———. 1978. *Pedagogy in Process*. New York: Continuum.

Gabelnick, F., J. MacGregor, R.S. Matthews, and B.L. Smith. 1990. *Learning Communities: Creating Connections Among Students, Faculty, and Disciplines*. New Directions for Teaching and Learning No. 41. San Francisco: Jossey-Bass.

Gaff, J.G., and S.S. Gaff. 1981. "Student-Faculty Relationships." In *The Modern American College*, edited by A.W. Chickering and Associates. San Francisco: Jossey-Bass.

Gamson, Z. 1991. "Five Takes on 'PC,' Diversity, and Community: The View from Student Affairs." *Change* 23(5): 40-47.

Gardner, H. 1993. *Multiple Intelligences: The Theory in Practice*. New York: Basic Books.

Gilligan, C. 1982. *In a Different Voice*. Cambridge, Mass.: Harvard University Press.

Giroux, H. 1983. *Theory and Resistance in Education: A Pedagogy for the Opposition*. Westport, Conn.: Greenwood, Bergin-Garvey.

———. 1988. *Schooling and the Struggle for Public Life: Critical Pedagogy in the Modern Age*. Minneapolis: University of Minnesota Press.

Glaser, B., and A. Strauss. 1967. *The Discovery of Grounded Theory*. Chicago: Aldine.

Goleman, D. 1995. *Emotional Intelligence*. New York: Bantam Books.

Good, T. 1987. "Two Decades of Research on Teacher Expectations: Findings and Future Directions." *Journal of Teacher Education* 38(6): 9-15.

Goodlad, J. 1984. *A Place Called School: Prospects for the Future*. New York: McGraw-Hill.

Goodsell, A. 1993. "Freshman Interest Groups: Linking Social and Academic Experiences of First-Year Students." Unpublished dissertation, Syracuse University.

Goodsell, A., M.R. Maher, V. Tinto, B.L. Smith, and J. MacGregor. 1992. *Collaborative Learning: A Sourcebook for Higher Education*. University Park, Pa.: National Center on Postsecondary Teaching, Learning, and Assessment. ED 357 705. 175 pp. MF-01; PC-07.

Gose, B. March 8, 1996. "Promoting Intellectual Life." *Chronicle of Higher Education*: A33-34.

Grant, G., and D. Riesman. 1978. *The Perpetual Dream: Reform and Experiment in the American College*. Chicago: University of Chicago Press.

Harnett, R.T. 1965. "Involvement in Extracurricular Activities as a Factor in Academic Performance." *Journal of College Student Personnel* 6: 272-74.

Hastorf, A.H., and A.M. Isen. 1982. *Cognitive Social Psychology*. New York: Elsevier.

Horowitz, H.L. 1987. *Campus Life: Undergraduate Cultures From the End of the Eighteenth Century to the Present*. Chicago: University of Chicago Press.

Jackson, B.T. 1993. Forward. In *In Search of Understanding: The Case for Constructivist Classrooms*, by J.G. Brooks and M.G. Brooks. Alexandria, Va.: Association for Supervision and Curriculum Development.

Jencks, C.S., and D. Riesman. 1962. "Patterns of Residential Education: A Case Study of Harvard." In *The American College: A Psychological and Social Interpretation of the Higher Learning*, edited by N. Sanford. New York: John Wiley and Sons.

Johnson, D.W., R.T. Johnson, and K.A. Smith. 1991. *Cooperative Learning: Increasing College Faculty Instructional Productivity*. ASHE-ERIC Higher Education Report No. 4. Washington, D.C.: Association for the Study of Higher Education. ED 343 465. 168 pp. MF-01; PC-07.

Johnson, D.W., G. Maruyama, R. Johnson, D. Nelson, and L. Skon. 1981. "Effects of Cooperative, Competitive, and Individualistic Goal Structures on Achievement: A Meta-analysis." *Psychological Bulletin* 89: 47-62.

Josselson, R. 1987. *Finding Herself: Pathways to Identity Development in Women*. San Francisco: Jossey-Bass.

Kadel, S., and J.A. Keehner. 1994. *Collaborative Learning: A Sourcebook for Higher Education*, vol. II. University Park, Pa.: National Center on Postsecondary Teaching, Learning, and Assessment.

Kagan, D.M. 1990. "How Schools Alienate Students at Risk: A

Model for Examining Proximal Classroom Variables."
Educational Psychologist 25: 105-25.

Katz, J. 1962. "Interpersonal Relations in the Classroom." In *The American College: A Psychological and Social Interpretation of the Higher Learning*, edited by N. Sanford. New York: John Wiley and Sons.

Katz, L.G. 1985. "Dispositions in Early Childhood Education." *ERIC/EECE Bulletin* 18: 2. Urbana, Ill.: ERIC Clearinghouse on Elementary and Early Childhood Education.

Kegan, R. 1982. *The Evolving Self: Problem and Process in Human Development*. Cambridge, Mass.: Harvard University Press.

Kennedy, D. 1995. "Another Century's End, Another Revolution for Higher Education." *Change* 27(3): 8-15.

Kilmann, R.H., M.J. Saxton, and R. Serpa. 1985. *Gaining Control of the Corporate Culture*. San Francisco: Jossey-Bass.

King, P.M. 1996. "Student Cognition and Learning." In *Student Services: A Handbook for the Profession,* 3d ed., by S.R. Komives, D.B. Woodard, and Associates. San Francisco: Jossey-Bass.

King, P.M., and K.S. Kitchener. 1994. *Developing Reflective Judgment: Understanding and Promoting Intellectual Growth and Critical Thinking in Adolescents and Adults*. San Francisco: Jossey-Bass.

King, P.M., and M.B. Baxter Magolda. 1996. "A Developmental Perspective on Learning." *Journal of College Student Development* 37: 163-73.

Kohlberg, L. 1971. "Stages of Moral Development." In *Moral Education*, edited by C.M. Beck, B.S. Crittendon, and E.V. Sullivan. Toronto: University of Toronto Press.

———. 1975. "Latest Version of the Theory of the Just Community School." Unpublished manuscript, Harvard University.

Kohn, A. 1986. *No Contest: The Case Against Competition*. Boston: Houghton Mifflin Co.

Kuh, G.D. 1993a. *Cultural Perspectives in Student Affairs Work*. Lanham, Md.: University Press of America.

———. 1993b. "In Their Own Words: What Students Learn Outside the Classroom." *American Educational Research Journal* 30: 277-304.

———. 1995. "The Other Curriculum: Out-of-Class Experiences Associated with Student Learning and Personal Development." *Journal of Higher Education* 66: 123-55.

Kuh, G.D., J.P. Bean, R.K. Bradley, and M.D. Coomes. 1986. "Contributions of Student Affairs Journals to the Literature on

College Students." *Journal of College Student Personnel* 27: 292-304.

Kuh, G.D., B. Douglas, J. Lund, and J. Ramin-Gyurnek. 1994. *Student Learning Outside the Classroom: Transcending Artificial Boundaries*. ASHE-ERIC Higher Education Report No. 8. Washington, D.C.: Association for the Study of Higher Education. HE 029 138. 163 pp. MF-01; PC-07.

Kuh, G.D., J. Schuh, E.J. Whitt, and Associates. 1991. *Involving Colleges*. San Francisco: Jossey-Bass.

Kuh, G.D., J.D. Shedd, and E.J. Whitt. 1987. "Student Affairs and Liberal Education: Unrecognized (and Unappreciated) Common Law Partners." *Journal of College Student Personnel* 28: 252-60.

Kuh, G.D., and E.J. Whitt. 1988. *The Invisible Tapestry: Culture in American Colleges and University*. ASHE-ERIC Higher Education Report No. 1. Washington, D.C.: Association for the Study of Higher Education. ED 299 934. 160 pp. MF-01; PC-07.

Kurfiss, J. 1983. *Intellectual, Psychological, and Moral Development in College: Four Major Theories*. Washington, D.C.: Council for Independent Colleges. ED 295 534. 44 pp. MF-01; PC-02.

Lamont, L. 1979. *Campus Shock: A Firsthand Report on College Life Today*. New York: E.P. Dulton.

Lawrenz, F.P. 1992. "Training the Teaching Assistants." *Journal of College Science Teaching* 22: 106-09.

Learning Communities Directory. 1995. Olympia, Wash.: Washington Center for Improving the Quality of Undergraduate Education.

Leemon, T.A. 1972. *The Rites of Passage in a Student Culture: A Study of the Dynamics of Transition*. New York: Teachers College Press.

Li, A.K.F. 1992. "Peer Relations and Social Skills Training: Implications for the Multicultural Classroom." *Journal of Educational Issues of Language Minority Students* 10: 67-78.

Lincoln, Y., and E. Guba. 1989. *Fourth Generation Evaluation*. Beverly Hills, Calif.: Sage.

Loevinger, J. 1976. *Ego Development: Conceptions and Theories*. San Francisco: Jossey-Bass.

Love, P. 1990. "An Investigation into the Organizational Culture of a Student Affairs Department." Unpublished doctoral dissertation, Indiana University.

Love, P., V.J. Boschini, B.A. Jacobs, C.M. Hardy, and G.D. Kuh. 1993. "Student Culture." In *Cultural Perspectives in Student Affairs Work*, edited by G.D. Kuh. Lanham, Md.: American College Personnel Association.

Love, P., G.D. Kuh, K.A. MacKay, and C.M. Hardy. 1993. "Side by Side: Faculty and Student Affairs Culture." In *Cultural Perspectives in Student Affairs Work*, edited by G.D. Kuh. Lanham, Md.: American College Personnel Association.

Lucas, C.J. 1985. "Out at the Edge: Notes on a Paradigm Shift." *Journal of Counseling and Development* 64: 165-72.

Lundeberg, M.A., and S. Diemert Moch. 1995. "Influence of Social Interaction on Cognition: Connected Learning in Science." *Journal of Higher Education* 66: 312-35.

Lyons, J.W. 1990. "Examining the Validity of Basic Assumptions and Beliefs." In *New Futures for Student Affairs: Building a Vision for Professional Leadership and Practice*, by M.J. Barr, M.L. Upcraft, and Associates. San Francisco: Jossey-Bass.

MacGregor, J. Fall 1991. "What Differences Do Learning Communities Make?" *Washington Center News* 6(1): 4-9. Olympia, Wash.: Washington Center for Improving the Quality of Undergraduate Education.

Manning, K. 1993. "Loosening the Ties that Bind: Shaping Student Culture." In *Cultural Perspectives in Student Affairs Work*, edited by G.D. Kuh. Lanham, Md.: University Press of America.

——. 1994. "Liberation Theology and Student Affairs." *Journal of College Student Development* 35: 94-97.

Matthews, R.S., J.L. Cooper, N. Davidson, and P. Hawkes. 1995. "Building Bridges Between Cooperative and Collaborative Learning." *Change* 27(4): 35-40.

McLaren, P. 1989. *Life in Schools: An Introduction to Critical Pedagogy in the Foundations of Education*. New York: Longman.

McLaren, P., and P. Leonard. 1993. *Paulo Freire: A Critical Encounter*. New York: Routledge.

Medley, D. 1979. "The Effectiveness of Teachers." In *Research on Teaching: Concepts, Findings and Implications*, edited by P.L. Peterson and H.J. Walberg. Berkeley, Calif.: McCutchan.

Merton, R.K. 1963. *Social Theory and Social Structure*. New York: Free Press.

Meyers, C., and T.B. Jones. 1993. *Promoting Active Learning: Strategies for the College Classroom*. San Francisco: Jossey-Bass.

Miller, T.K., and J.D. Jones. 1981. "Out-of-Class Activities." In *The Modern American College*, edited by A.W. Chickering and Associates. San Francisco: Jossey-Bass.

Miller, T.K., and J.S. Prince. 1976. *The Future of Student Affairs*. San Francisco: Jossey-Bass.

Mitchell, A.A., and M. Roof. 1989. "Student Affairs and Faculty

Partnerships: Dismantling Barriers." *NASPA Journal* 26: 278-83.

Moffatt, M. 1989. *Coming of Age in New Jersey: College and American Culture*. New Brunswick, N.J.: Rutgers University Press.

Monaghan, P. June 7, 1989. "Unusual Washington State Clearinghouse Develops Teaching and Learning Innovations for Colleges." *Chronicle of Higher Education*: A11-13.

Mueller, K.H. 1961. *Student Personnel Work in Higher Education*. Boston: Houghton Mifflin.

Murguia, E., R.V. Padilla, and M. Pavel. 1991. "Ethnicity and the Concept of Social Integration in Tinto's Model of Institutional Departure." *Journal of College Student Development* 32: 433-39.

Murphy, J.F., M. Weil, P. Hallinger, and A. Mitman. 1982. "Academic Press: Translating High Expectations into School Policies and Classroom Practices." *Educational Leadership* 40(3): 22-26.

National Association of Student Personnel Administrators. 1987. *A Perspective on Student Affairs*. Washington, D.C.

Newcomb, T.M. 1943. *Personality and Social Change: Attitude Formation in a Student Community*. New York: Dryden Press.

———. 1962. "Student Peer Group Influence." In *The American College: A Psychological and Social Interpretation of the Higher Learning*, edited by N. Sanford. New York: John Wiley and Sons.

Newcomb, T.M., and E. Wilson. 1966. *College Peer Groups*. Chicago: Aldine.

Nyquist, J.D. 1989. *Teaching Assistant Training in the 1990s*. New Directions for Teaching and Learning No. 39. San Francisco: Jossey-Bass.

O'Keefe, B.J., and J.G. Delia. 1982. "Impression Formation and Message Production." In *Social Cognition and Communication*, edited by M.E. Roloff and C.R. Berger. Beverly Hills, Calif.: Sage.

Ory, J.C., and L.A. Braskamp. 1988. "Involvement and Growth of Students in Three Academic Programs." *Research in Higher Education* 28: 116-29.

Pace, R. 1987. "Good Things Go Together. Project on the Student of Quality in Undergraduate Education." Los Angeles: Higher Education Research Institute, University of California.

Page, R.M., and T.S. Page. 1993. *Fostering Emotional Well-Being in the Classroom*. Boston: Jones and Bartlett.

Palmer, P.J. 1983. *To Know as We Are Known: Education as a Spiritual Journey*. San Francisco: Harper.

———. 1987. "Community, Conflict, and Ways of Knowing: Ways to Deepen Our Educational Agenda." *Change* 19(5): 20-25.

———. 1990. "Good Teaching: A Matter of Living the Mystery." *Change* 22(1): 11-16.

Pascarella, E., and P.T. Terenzini. 1980. "Student-Faculty and Student Peer Relationships as Mediators of the Structural Effects of Undergraduate Residence Arrangement." *Journal of Educational Research* 73: 344-53.

———. 1981. "Residence Arrangement, Student/Faculty Relationships, and Freshman-Year Educational Outcomes." *Journal of College Student Personnel* 22: 147-56.

———. 1991. *How College Affects Students*. San Francisco: Jossey-Bass.

Pascarella, E., P.T. Terenzini, and G.S. Blimling. 1994. "The Impact of Residential Life on Students." In *Realizing the Educational Potential of Residence Halls*, edited by C.C. Schroeder and P. Mable. San Francisco: Jossey-Bass.

Perkins, D., E. Jay, and S. Tishman. 1994. "The National Assessment of College Student Learning: Identification of the Skills to Be Taught, Learned, and Assessed." Report on the proceedings of the Second Study Design Workshop. Washington, D.C.: U.S. Department of Education, Office of Educational Research and Improvement. Document no. NCES 94-286. ED 372 717. 321 pp. MF-01; PC-13.

Perry, W.G. Jr. 1970. *Forms of Intellectual and Ethical Development in the College Years*. New York: Holt, Rinehart & Winston.

———. 1981. "Cognitive and Ethical Growth: The Making of Meaning." In *The Modern American College*, edited by A.W. Chickering. San Francisco: Jossey-Bass.

Peterson, C., and M.E.P. Seligman. 1984. "Causal Explanations as a Risk Factor for Depression: Theory and Evidence." *Psychological Review* 91: 347-74.

Piaget, J.R. 1926. *The Language and Thought of the Child*. New York: Harcourt, Brace and Co.

———. 1928. *Judgment and Reasoning in the Child*. New York: Harcourt, Brace and Co.

———. 1969. *Science of Education and the Psychology of the Child*. New York: Viking Compass.

Piaget, J.R., and B. Inhelder. 1971. *Psychology of the Child*. New York: Basic Books.

Polkosnik, M.C., and R.B. Winston Jr. 1989. "Relationships Between Students' Intellectual and Psychosocial Development: An Exploratory Investigation." *Journal of College Student Development* 30: 10-19.

Poole, J.R. 1991. "Seven Skills to Improve Teaching: Enhancing

Graduate Assistant Instruction." *Journal of Physical Education, Recreation, and Dance* 62: 21-24.

Reger, M.P., and R. Hyman. 1988. "Academic and Student Affairs: Perceptions on Partnerships." *NASPA Journal* 26: 64-70.

Rendon, L. 1992. *From the Barrio to the Academy: Revelations of a Mexican American 'Scholarship Girl.' First-Generation Students: Confronting Cultural Issues.* New Directions for Community Colleges No. 80. San Francisco: Jossey-Bass.

Rhoads, R.A., and M.A. Black. 1995. "'Student Affairs Practitioners as Transformative Educators: Advancing a Critical Cultural Perspective." *Journal of College Student Development* 36: 413-21.

Rice, R.E., and H.W. Sheridan. April 1989. "Tomorrow's Professoriate: The Search for a New Vision." Paper presented at the annual conference of the American Association of Higher Education, Chicago.

Romer, K.T. 1985. "Collaboration: New Forms of Learning, New Ways of Thinking." *The Forum for Liberal Education* 8(2): 2-18.

Rosen, L.M. 1992. "Valuing the Collaborative, Language-Centered Classroom: What Theorists and Teachers Tell Us." Paper presented at the annual meeting of the Conference on College Composition and Communication, Cincinnati. ED 345 251. 14 pp. MF-01; PC-01.

Roueche, J.E., and G.A. Baker. 1987. *Access and Excellence: The Open Door College.* Washington, D.C.: The Community College Press.

Roueche, J.E., and S.D. Roueche. 1994. "Creating the Climate for Teaching and Learning." In *Teaching and Learning in the Community College*, edited by T. O'Banion. Washington, D.C.: Community College Press.

Rubin, R.A., and S.A. Henzl. 1984. "Cognitive Complexity, Communication Competence, and Verbal Ability." *Communication Quarterly* 32(4): 263-70.

Russo, P. 1995. "Struggling for Knowledge: Students, Community College, and Learning Communities." Unpublished dissertation, Syracuse University.

Ryan, M. 1995. "The Collegiate Way: Historical Purposes of Residential Colleges." *Talking Stick* 12(7): 8-16.

Salovey, P., and J.D. Mayer. 1990. "Emotional Intelligence." *Imagination, Cognition, and Personality* 9: 185-211.

Schein, E.H. 1985. *Organizational Culture and Leadership.* San Francisco: Jossey-Bass.

Schniedewind, N., and E. Davidson. 1987. *Cooperative Learning, Cooperative Lives: A Sourcebook of Learning Activities for*

Building a Peaceful World. Dubuque, Iowa: William C. Brown.

Schroeder, C.C., and J.C. Hurst. 1996. "Designing Learning Environments that Integrate Curricular and Cocurricular Experiences." *Journal of College Student Development* 37: 174-81.

Schroeder, C.C., J.K. DiTiberio, and D.H. Kalsbeek. 1988. "Bridging the Gap Between Faculty and Students: Opportunities and Obligations for Student Affairs." *NASPA Journal* 26(1): 14-20.

Seiler, W.J. 1989. *Communication in the Contemporary Classroom.* New York: Holt, Reinhart and Winston.

Shaffer, R.H. 1993. "Whither Student Personnel Work from 1968 to 2018?: A 1993 Retrospective." *NASPA Journal* 30(3): 162-68.

Shor, I. 1992. *Empowering Education: Critical Teaching for Social Change.* Chicago: University of Chicago Press.

———. 1993. "Education Is Politics: Paulo Freire's Critical Pedagogy." In *Paulo Freire: A Critical Encounter,* edited by P. McLaren and P. Leonard. New York: Routledge.

Shott, S. 1979. "Emotion and Social Life: A Symbolic Interactionist Perspective." *American Journal of Sociology* 84: 1,317-34.

Slavin, R.E. 1989-90. "Research on Cooperative Learning: Consensus and Controversy." *Educational leadership* 47(4): 52-55.

Smith, B.L., and J.T. MacGregor. 1992. "What is Collaborative Learning?" In *Collaborative Learning: A Sourcebook for Higher Education,* edited by A.S. Goodsell, M.R. Maher, V. Tinto, B.L. Smith, and J.T. MacGregor. University Park, Pa.: National Center on Postsecondary Teaching, Learning, and Assessment. ED 357 705. 175 pp. MF-01; PC-07.

Smith, D.G. 1988. "A Window of Opportunity for Intra-Institutional Collaboration." *NASPA Journal* 26: 8-13.

Smith, T.B., and E. Raney (1993). *The North American Directory of Residential Colleges and Living Learning Centers.* Kirksville, Mo.: Northeast Missouri State University.

Smith-Lovin, L. 1989. "Sentiment, Affect, and Emotion." *Socialpsychology Quarterly* 52(1): v-xii.

Sommers, S. 1982. "Social Cognition, Nonsocial Cognition, and Interpersonal Processes in Adulthood." Paper presented at the annual meeting of the Eastern Psychological Association, Baltimore. ED 221 812. 18 pp. MF-01; PC-01.

Springer, L., P.T. Terenzini, E.T. Pascarella, and A. Nora. 1995. "Influences on College Students' Orientations Toward Learning for Self-Understanding." *Journal of College Student Development* 36(1): 5-18.

Stage, F.K. 1996. "Setting the Context: Psychological Theories of

Learning." *Journal of College Student Development* 37: 227-35.

Stein, J. 1995. "Recognizing the Educational Potential of Residential Communities." *Talking Stick* 12(7): 26-27.

Strauss, A., and J. Corbin. 1990. *Basics of Qualitative Research: Grounded Theory Procedures and Techniques*. Newbury Park, Calif.: Sage.

Stringer, J., B.M. Steckler, and D.R. Johnson. 1988. "Collaborative Approaches to Student Growth From the Student Life and Academic Sectors." *NASPA Journal* 26(1): 45-53.

'Student Focus' Stressed at Muhlenberg. October 26, 1994. *Chronicle of Higher Education*: A39-A41.

Study Group on the Conditions of Excellence in American Higher Education. 1984. "Involvement in Learning: Realizing the Potential of American Higher Education." Washington, D.C.: National Institute of Education. ED 246 833. 127 pp. MF-01; PC-06.

Sylvester, R. 1994. "How Emotions Affect Learning." *Educational Leadership* 52: 60-65.

Terenzini, P.T., K.W. Allison, S.B. Millar, L.I. Rendon, M.L. Upcraft, P. Gregg, and R. Jalomo. 1992. "The Transition to College Project: Final Report." University Park, Pa.: National Center on Postsecondary Teaching, Learning, and Assessment.

Thayer, R.E. 1989. *The Biopsychology of Mood and Arousal*. New York: Oxford University Press.

Tiberius, R.G., and J.M. Billson. 1991. "The Social Context of Teaching and Learning." In *College Teaching: From Theory to Practice*, edited by R.J. Menges and M.D. Svinicki. New Directions for Teaching and Learning No. 45. San Francisco: Jossey-Bass.

Tierney, W.G. 1990. *Assessing Academic Climates and Cultures*. New Directions for Institutional Research No. 68. San Francisco: Jossey-Bass.

———. 1993. *Building Communities of Difference: Higher Education in the Twenty-First Century*. Westport, Conn.: Bergin and Garvey.

Tierney, W.G., and R.A. Rhoads. 1994. *Faculty Socialization as Cultural Process: A Mirror of Institutional Commitment*. ASHE-ERIC Higher Education Report No. 6. Washington, D.C.: The Association for the Study of Higher Education. ED 368 322. 123 pp. MF-01; PC-05.

Tinto, V. 1993. *Leaving College: Rethinking the Causes and Cures of Student Attrition*. 2d ed. Chicago: University of Chicago Press.

Tinto, V., and A. Goodsell. 1993. "Freshman Interest Groups and the First-year Experience: Constructing Student Communities in a Large University." *Journal of the Freshman Year Experience* 6(1): 7-28.

Tinto, V., A. Goodsell Love, and P. Russo. 1993. "Building Community." *Liberal Education* 79(4): 16-21.

———. 1994. *Building Learning Communities for New College Students.* University Park, Pa.: National Center on Postsecondary Teaching, Learning, and Assessment.

Tinto, V., P. Russo, and S. Kadel. 1994. "Constructing Educational Communities: Increasing Retention in Challenging Circumstances." *American Association of Community Colleges Journal* 64: 26-29.

Van Maanen, J. 1976. "Breaking In: Socialization to Work." In *Handbook of Work, Organization, and Society,* edited by R. Dubin. Chicago: Rand McNally College Publishing.

———. 1984. "Doing New Things in Old Ways: The Chains of Socialization." In *College and University Organization: Insights From the Behavioral Sciences,* edited by J.L. Bess. New York: New York University Press.

Von Bertalanffy, L. 1969. *General Systems Theory: Foundations, Development, Applications.* New York: G. Braziller.

Weinstein, R. 1989. "Perceptions of Classroom Processes and Student Motivation: Children's Views of Self-Fulfilling Prophecies." In *Research on Motivation in Education, vol. 3: Goals and Cognition,* edited by C. Ames and R. Ames. San Diego: Academic Press.

Wiener, H.S. 1986. "Collaborative Learning in the Classroom: A Guide to Evaluation." *College English* 48(1): 52-61.

Wilkins, A.L., and K.J. Patterson. 1986. "You Can't Get There From Here: What Will Make Culture Change Projects Fail." In *Gaining Control of the Corporate Culture,* edited by R.H. Kilmann, M. Saxton, R. Serpa, and Associates. San Francisco: Jossey-Bass.

Williamson, E.G. July 1957. "The Dean of Students as Educator." *The Educational Record*: 230-40.

———. 1961. *Student Personnel Services in College and Universities.* New York: McGraw-Hill.

Ziegler, S. 1981. "The Effectiveness of Cooperative Learning Teams for Increasing Cross-Ethnic Friendship: Additional Evidence." *Human Organization* 40(3): 264-68.

INDEX

A

AAHE. See American Association for Higher Education

academic

achievement and cognitive development associated with
high levels of hope, optimism and impulse control, 47

advisors role, 87–88

belief system subordinated nonintellectual activities to
rational, empirically based knowledge, 10

development more than just intellectual development, 7

learning communities as linked pairs of classes or clusters
of courses linked by an integrating seminar, 82

separation from out-of-classroom experiences,
reasons for, ix-x

active learning. See also collaborative learning

comprehensive sources on, 60–61

acts of profound love

required by those who benefit most from a system to
dismantle and transform it, 64

alternative pedagogies emphasize

student experience as starting point for student learning, 55

American Association for Higher Education, 84

promoting Continuous Quality Improvement merging with
assessment movement, 27

American Philosophical Association

consensual description of critical thinking of, 35

anticipatory socialization, 94

anti-intellectual student culture, 22

fosters fragmentation of intellectual, emotional and social
elements of learning, 53

art of praxis required by new teaching concepts, 63–64

assessment

movement as result of external pressures, 27

need for social and emotional influences on learning, 67–68

Astin (1993)

traditional-aged students culture dominated by desires for
self-fulfillment, 22

B

banking model of education, 45

barriers

between faculty and student affairs professionals, 19

to student learning requires new teaching concepts, 62

Brubacher and Rudy (1976), 11–12
Bruffee (1993)
> best resource about collaborative learning, 60

Buerck (1985)
> assesses of social and emotional influences and outcomes in natural sciences and mathematics, 67

C

campus living
> enhanced amount of social interaction students had with faculty and peers, 92

campus or academic community
> calls for a more unified, 23

Cartesian influence dominant in natural science, 25

catalysts for reform in higher education, 99–100

Chickering and Gamson (1987)
> Seven Practices for Good Practice in Undergraduate Education of, 67

Chickering and Reisser (1993)
> assignments that invite engaging emotionally as well as intellectually can assist with emotion management, 37
> intellectual activity is an effective avenue to incorporate work on social and emotional development, 68
> relationships provide powerful learning experiences and opportunities to enhance cognitive development, 31
> ways to maximize intellectual, social and emotional developmental influence of residence-hall living, 92–93

classrooms
> comparison of traditional and constructivist, 48
> lack of positive emotions in, 34

cognitive development
> how student social and emotional needs can be used as catalysts for, 58
> social aspects not often given credit, 30
> theorists, 95
> works: Perry (1970), Kohlberg (1971), and Gilligan (1982), 21

cognitive dissonance as a precursor to learning, 30

cognitively complex
> more likely will holistically perceive interacting situation and contexts, 40

Collaboration in Undergraduate Education Network
> subgroup of American Association for Higher Education, 84

Constructivism

knowledge as temporary, developmental, socially and culturally mediated and thus nonobjective, 47

focus on interactionist aspect of Piaget's work knowledge comes from interaction and unity of learning and learner, 49

Constructivist Pedagogy, 6, 47–50

celebrates the complexity of the known world, 47

cooperative learning as a practical extension of, 58

emphasis on learning rather than right answers, 48

contextual knowing

cognitive development integrating relational and impersonal knowing, 40

Continuous Quality Improvement movement, 27

cooperation superior to competition

in terms of achievement and feelings of well-being, 30

cooperative learning

as a practical extension of constructivist pedagogy, 58

promotes idea that acquiring and creating knowledge is an active social process students need to practice, 57

similar to but not same as collaborative learning, 57

strategies often incorporate the use of small groups of students working toward a common educational goal, 57

coordinated studies program, 83

core requirements

call for consistency and coherence through general-education, 26–27

critical consciousness as the ultimate goal of education in liberation theory, 46

Critical Cultural Perspective, 50–53

like liberation theory in that requires mutual debate and discourse about issues, 51

strength and embeddedness of current culture and subcultures are recognized, 51

should be used in teaching in student affairs graduate preparation programs, 95–96

Cross and Angelo (1992)

classroom assessment techniques with own teaching as an object of scholarship, 26

CUE. See Collaboration in Undergraduate Education

culturally sensitive educators required with new teaching concepts, 63

culture change assessment requires sustained detailed study, 100

D

deans of men and women

as new positions created to supervise non-academic life of students, 16

Descartes, Rene

writings espoused the split between mind and body, 10

development interrelatedness

cognitive, social, and affective elements of, 40

disequilibrium as precursor to learning, 30

division of labor between faculty and student affairs needs to be "softened," 6

doctoral programs must play a significant role in changing faculty culture, 94

Dorsey, Marlene

thanked for reviewing drafts of this report, xiii

Do "with" students rather than doing "for students

new teaching concepts requires, 62

Duke University

changes initiated in an attempt to promote intellectual life of campus, 99

E

education

as a victory of form over substance, 49–50

purpose of academic, 9

system as one of major instruments for maintenance of culture, 44–45

Eliot, President of Harvard College

oversaw dismantling of rigid set of course requirements for undergraduates, 12

emotional abilities can enhance cognitive abilities and academic achievement, 37

emotional development

process through which students become aware of emotions, learn to

manage and incorporate them into overall development, 7

emotional influences include internal affective states and negative feeling states, 7

Emotional Intelligences model

includes recognizing emotions in others and managing relationships, 38

emotional states and social performance in the classroom

strong relationship between, 39

emotion management assistance
> through assignments that engage emotionally as well as intellectually, 37

emotions important in education because
> drives attention which [in turn] drives learning and memory, 36

Estanek, Sandy
> thanked for reviewing drafts of this report, xiii

ethos of holistic learning
> tactics toward providing, 79

The Evergreen State College
> coordinated studies programs at, 84

Experimental College curriculum, 15

"Experiment at Berkeley," 15

F

faculty
> benefits from sole focus on intellectual activity, 3
>
> culture discussion in: Tierney (1990) and Tierney and Rhoads (1994), 19
>
> must be seen as emotional and social beings, 61
>
> perceive student affairs professionals as providing only for basic needs, 19–20
>
> provided with little on the nature and structure of academic organizations, 20
>
> receive little training in teaching, 20
>
> tend to emphasize content, 1
>
> value autonomy of collaboration, 20
>
> value thinking and reflecting over doing, 20

faculty and student affairs professionals
> barriers due to orientation differences between, 19
>
> intentional influencing orientation of, 93–97

faculty members
> benefits of collaborative learning process for, 59–60

faculty need in order to stimulate change
> to bring to a conscious level tacit understandings of student culture, 55

faculty reward and support systems
> need to support collaborative and cross-disciplinary work, 91

Fassinger (1995)
> strong relationship between emotional states and social performance in the classroom, 39

fear as inhibitor of creative conflict in the classroom, 40–41 feelings and intellect

description of interrelatedness of, 35

Feldman and Newcomb (1969)

choreographing of intellectual with emotional and interpersonal development has greatest impact on students, ix

field sensitive learners relying on extrinsic stimuli to facilitate
learning, 33

FIGs. See Freshman interest groups

foreclosure (state of premature resolution), supportive role in
moving beyond, 32

Freire (1970), Pedagogy of the Oppressed, 44

acts of profound love required for those who benefit most
from a system to dismantle and transform it, 64

everyday actions serve to perpetuate cultural systems, 72

Freshman interest groups, 84–86

courses of, 84

G

Gamson (1991)

must be able to feel the learning and then have opportunity
for growth, 35

Gardner (1993)

positive home environment creates positive effect on social
and psychological well being leading to higher academic
achievement, 39–40

theory of multiple intelligences, 38

German university model

compelled faculty members to specialize in particular
discipline, 12

shift to, 11

Gilligan (1982)

work related to cognitive development, 21

Goleman (1995)

academic achievement and cognitive development with
high levels of hope, optimism and impulse control, 47

description of interrelatedness of feelings and intellect, 35

emotional skills better predictors of various measures of
academic success than was IQ, 37

Goodlad (1984)

lack of positive emotions in the classroom, 34

Goodsell, Maher, Tinto, Smith, and MacGregor (1992)

collaborative learning resources, 60

grade emphasis of students

because of determinant of desirable residence rather than from concern with intellectual development, 22

"Great Books," use of , 15

greater social harmony as reason why institutions should develop a more comprehensive approach to their education process, x

"Grinds." See "Outsiders

H

Harvard College

history of adoption of German university model, 12–13

Harvard House System, 14

higher education

may be reaching a bifurcation point, 76–77

professionals must become a more direct influence in the lives of students, 54

"higher-education culture"

assumes that moral and ethical development not in purview of educators, 21

Kuh and Whitt (1988) discussion of, 19

of individualism which mirrors positivism world view, 26

term misleading because of assertion that there is a single culture, 18

high expectations for students results

in higher self-esteem and higher self-concept concerning ability, 65

Historf and Isen (1982)

difficulties in dealing with affect and cognitive development, 34

Hoffman, Nancy

contributed to understanding of authors, xiii

holistic student learning

definition of, 6

factors that contributed to disintegration of a sense of, 16

focus results, 100

perspective should be expected in internship and assistantships experiences of

student affairs graduate preparation programs, 96

higher education must move in direction of, 99

Horowitz (1987), Campus Life: Undergraduate Cultures From the End of the

intellectual

>   activity as a means of incorporating work on social and
>   emotional development, 68

>   development enhanced by a willingness to ask questions
>   and add to discussion, 32

intelligence functioning

>   emotions as energetic source for, 35–36

interest as vital affective state in process of knowledge construction
>   among children, 49

interpersonal intelligence

>   better able to perceive and respond to others with higher
>   degree of, 38

interpersonal relationships between teachers and students
>   research emphasis in the 1960s on, 25

involvement

>   methods to promote, 82

"Involving Colleges"

>   study, 33

>   theme of reduction or elimination in the use of titles , 62–63

IQ scores can be raised by emotional abilities, 37

J

Jencks and Riesman (1962)

>   provide description of Harvard House System, 14

Josselson (1987)

>   identified the role of supportive people in moving beyond
>   foreclosure, 32

K

Kadel and Keehner (1994)

>   collaborative learning resources, 60

Katz (1962)

>   use of psychological term transference to describe
>   interactions between students and faculty, 25

King and Baxter Magolda (1996)

>   constructing and use of knowledge closely tied to sense of
>   self, 35

>   interrelatedness of cognitive, social, and affective elements
>   of development, 40

King and Kitchener (1994)

>   cognitive development theorist whose work is incorporated
>   in student affairs preparation programs, 95

knowledge

under attack by new philosophies, 44

liberal arts model of education, 11

liberation theology

as a better name for liberation theory, 47

Liberation Theory, 6, 44–47

adoption requires a critical cultural perspective, 51

everyone learns from everyone else in, 46

focus on bringing students' emotional & social experiences to learning process, 47

should be in student affairs graduate preparation programs, 95

lists of objectives for overhauling general education have remarkable resemblance's, 27

Living Learning Centers, 6, 89–90

as a means to encourage student-faculty contact, 71

incorporate learning activities with living arrangements, 82

linking takes place through the social element of the living space, 89

listing of institutions with such programs, 89

living on campus

not clearly enhancing for all aspects of learning and development, 91–92

Love, Kuh, MacKay and Hardy (1993)

student affairs professionals,

unlike faculty, focused both on basic and higher order needs, 19

Lowell, Abbott Lawrence

Harvard President who tried influencing peer culture toward intellectual ends, 14

Lucas (1985)

writes about paradigm shifts in natural and social sciences, 24–25

Lundeberg and Diemert Moch (1995)

emphasis on connected knowing through collaborative supplemental instruction increased student success, 32

on assessment of social and emotional influences and outcomes in natural sciences and mathematics, 67

M

Magolda (1992)

cognitive development theorist whose work is incorporated in student affairs preparation programs, 95

satisfying human relationships as a necessary but
insufficient condition for student learning, 66

N

National Council for Teachers of Mathematics and National Science
Teachers Association endorsed movement away from a
quest for answers and toward a search for processes, 50

Newcomb (1943)
studied attitudes of students at Bennington College
between 1935 and 1939, 14–15

Newcomb (1962)
study of interaction within a student peer groups, 15

Newcomb and Wilson (1966)
spheres of peer group and those of the intellect overlap
only slightly, 22

new disciplines
as part of a larger paradigm shift in education, 26

New Mexico
use of "Great Books" at, 15

O

O'Keefe and Delia (1982)
more cognitively complex then more likely will holistically
perceive interacting situation and contexts, 40

Organizational structure as reason for separation of academic from
out-of-classroom experiences, ix

out-of-class experiences
dramatic increase in recognition of influence on student
learning, 78
reasons for separation from academic experiences, ix-x
student-faculty contact as a way of focusing on the
individual student, 69
student-faculty interaction consistently shown to be very
influential in student growth and outcomes, 31

"Outsiders"
term for students intent on their studies, 13

P

Pace (1987)
those who benefit most intellectually from the college
experience also seem to benefit more in the affective- and
social development domains, 39

Page and Page (1993)

interest as vital affective state in process of knowledge
construction among children, 49

Polkosnik and Winston (1989)

little work directed toward gaining understanding of
integration of cognitive and psychosocial developments in
the individual, 4–5

Poock, Michael

thanked for reviewing drafts of this report, xiii

positive classroom climate

facilitates learning and therefore enhances students'
academic achievement, 38

positive paradigm

forced emotional and social processes out of the classroom,
11

has increasingly come under attack, 24–26

nothing is knowable except as it is susceptible to empirical
demonstration, 10

praxis

as reflection and action upon the world to transform it, 45

eaching required by new teaching concepts, 63–64

predictors of academic success

emotional skills better than IQ as, 37

process of thinking

context and social dimension of thinking influences the,
32–33

professional hierarchy on most campuses is invidious because

emphasizes intellectual development as higher and proper
ground for faculty, 18

Professors

trained to transmit knowledge and skills, not help students
become more mature, 2

psychology

early emphasis on behavior as the only objective
observable in the field, 25

psychosocial theories of development

citation of works on, 38

Q

qualitative studies of student experience

past decade has seen a significant increase in the number
of, 25

questionnaire use at beginning of class to learn about students, 69

R

Rational-Emotive Therapy, 36

reflection

on one's own socialization required by new teaching concepts, 62

on practices that maintain status and power differences between students, faculty and administration required by new teaching concepts, 62–63

on relationship with students and what role of social and emotional elements in teaching means for faculty, 70

registrar role in learning community planning, 88

relationships

provide powerful learning experiences and opportunities to enhance cognitive development, 31

types important for learning in an academic setting, 31

researchers and faculty practitioners

view that focuses efforts on students' intellectual and cognitive development, 4

Residence Halls

"major causal mechanism" for enhanced outcomes for students in, 92

need to enhance educational climate of, 91–93

ways to maximize intellectual, social and emotional influence of, 92–93

Rhoads and Black (1995)

critical cultural perspective compared to liberation theory in that requires mutual debate and discourse about issues, 51

Rosen (1992)

identified social, affective, and cognitive influences of collaborative learning, 58

Roueche and Baker (1987)

excellent instructors have an integrated perception of their students, 67

study of Miami-Dade Community College, 65–67

Russo, Pat

contributed to understanding of authors, xiii

Rutgers University (1989)

Moffatt's study at, 15

S

Salovay and Mayer's (1990)

model of Emotional Intelligences includes recognizing emotions in others and managing relationships, 38 scholarly activity

    effective integration, application and communication of knowledge as well as discovery or creation now part of, 26

scholarship

    emerging new and broader definitions of, 26

    redefining of, 20

Seattle Central Community College

    collaborative learning at, 59–60

    example of coordinated studies program at, 83

Self-Organizing systems

    process by which systems spontaneously become more complex when no longer able incorporate inputs, 75

Self-Organizing Theory, 75–77

senior tutor

    junior faculty member in Harvard House System, 14

separation of intellectual from emotional and social development

    objectives at larger institutions rationale, ix

Seven Principles of Good Practice in Undergraduate Education, 67, 72

Shott (1979)

    emotions as socially constructed, 38

Smith, Caryl Kelley

    acknowledge support of, xiii

Smith (1988)

    concerned that institutions are limiting student learning opportunities by separating classroom learning and life experience, 77

Smith and Raney (1993), The North American Directory of Residential Colleges and Living Learning Centers, 89

Smith-Lovin (1989)

    feelings always are interpreted in a social milieu, 38

social and intellectual development

    barriers to bridging of, 23

social cognition

    premised on belief that learning occurs in a social context, 31

social community on campus breakdown

    changes that contributed to a breakdown of, 10

social context

    most learning development takes place within, 30

social development

    definition of, 7

social deviations decreased as reason why institutions should develop a more comprehensive approach to their education process, x

role in implementation of classroom-based learning
communities, 86–89

role in training peer advisors, 88–89

should adopt liberation theory as a professional
philosophy, 70–71

strategies and actions in implementing liberation theory, 71

value collaboration over autonomy, 20

value doing over thinking and reflecting, 20

view urging faculty promotion of intellectual development
outside of classroom, 4

student affairs professionals need to

apply the Seven Principles of Good Practice in
Undergraduate Education, 71–72

assess intellectual and cognitive development as part of
out-of-class experiences, 71

be an intentional presence in students' intellectual lives,
72–73

encourage active learning, prompt feedback, workshops
use, and communication of high expectations, 72

participate in academically related activities, 56

respect diverse talents through support for pluralistic
communities, 72

student association of intellectual and cognitive knowledge
acquisition

with experiences in classroom, and laboratories rather than
out-of-classroom, 78

student culture

change requires faculty to bring to a conscious level tacit
understandings of, 55

faculty influence in shaping, 54–56

Horowitz (1987) discussion of, 19

influenced by student affairs professionals, 56–57

influences motivations, attitudes, values and beliefs about
learning that students carry with them into classroom, 29

of traditional-aged students dominated by desires for self-
fulfillment,

self-enhancement and financial security, 22

student demographic changes

as a potential barrier to integration of intellectual, emotional
and social process in learning process, 27–28

student development specialists tend to emphasize process, 1

student distrust of changes must recognize and deal with, 64

supportive climate

       prevents emotional overload by defining personal decorum, 66

supportive people role in

       moving beyond foreclosure (state of premature resolution), 32

Sylvester (1994)

       emotions important in education because drives attention which drives learning and memory, 36

T

teaching assistant training programs

       importance of, 94

teaching process

       importance of incorporating social and emotional elements in, 68

Terenzini and Pascarella (1991)

       integrative study concludes choreographing of intellectual with emotional and interpersonal development has greatest impact on students, ix

theory of multiple intelligences, 38

Tierney (1990) and Tierney and Rhoads (1994) discussion

       of faculty culture, 19

Tierney (1993)

       speaks of communities of differences as valued and to be nurtured, 23

Tinto, Vincent

       mentorship of, xiii

Tinto (1993)

       important to nurture many student subcultures within a single institution, 23

       link between social integration and retention and success, 3

Tompkins, Dan

       contributed to understanding of authors, xiii

Total Quality Management strategy

       as a model for integrating elements of student learning, 80

transference

       interactions between students and faculty, 25

Transformation

       requires trust, persistence and confidence in ultimate outcome, 64

tutor

       as graduate students in Harvard House System, 14

U

unified campus community

as barrier to bridging students' social, emotional, and
intellectual development, 23

University at Stony Brook

as an example of an integrated living-learning program, 89,
89–90

University of Washington

Freshman interest groups at, 84–85

University of Wisconsin

curricular reform efforts at, 15

V

value examination felt not purview of educators, 21

value-free content of the disciplines

safer for faculty than topics such as morals and values, 21

Van Bertalanffy (1969) described concept of self-organizing systems

as process by which systems spontaneously become more
complex

when no longer able incorporate inputs, 75

Van Der Karr, Carol

thanked for reviewing drafts of this report, xiii

Villanueva, Myrna

authors thank for help, xiii

visionary, persistent and pervasive leadership

needed for developing an ethos of holistic learning, 79–80

W

Washington Center for Improving the Quality of Undergraduate
Education, 84

Williams, Lee

thanked for reviewing drafts of this report, xiii

women value connectedness or social relationships in learning
experiences

to a greater extent than do men, 32

ASHE-ERIC HIGHER EDUCATION REPORTS

Since 1983, the Association for the Study of Higher Education (ASHE) and the Educational Resources Information Center (ERIC) Clearinghouse on Higher Education, a sponsored project of the Graduate School of Education and Human Development at The George Washington University, have cosponsored the ASHE-ERIC Higher Education Report series. The 1995 series is the twenty-fourth overall and the seventh to be published by the Graduate School of Education and Human Development at The George Washington University.

Each monograph is the definitive analysis of a tough higher education problem, based on thorough research of pertinent literature and institutional experiences. Topics are identified by a national survey. Noted practitioners and scholars are then commissioned to write the reports, with experts providing critical reviews of each manuscript before publication.

Eight monographs (10 before 1985) in the ASHE-ERIC Higher Education Report series are published each year and are available on individual and subscription bases. To order, use the order form on the last page of this book.

Qualified persons interested in writing a monograph for the ASHE-ERIC Higher Education Report series are invited to submit a proposal to the National Advisory Board. As the preeminent literature review and issue analysis series in higher education, the Higher Education Reports are guaranteed wide dissemination and national exposure for accepted candidates. Execution of a monograph requires at least a minimal familiarity with the ERIC database, including *Resources in Education* and the *Current Index to Journals in Education.* The objective of these reports is to bridge conventional wisdom with practical research. Prospective authors are strongly encouraged to call Dr. Fife at 800-773-3742.

For further information, write to
   ASHE-ERIC Higher Education Reports
   The George Washington University
   One Dupont Circle, Suite 630
   Washington, DC 20036
Or phone (202) 296-2597; toll free: 800-773-ERIC.

Write or call for a complete catalog.

ADVISORY BOARD

James Earl Davis
University of Delaware at Newark

Susan Frost
Emory University

Mildred Garcia
Montclair State College

James Hearn
University of Georgia

Bruce Anthony Jones
University of Pittsburgh

L. Jackson Newell
Deep Springs College

Carolyn Thompson
State University of New York-Buffalo

CONSULTING EDITORS

Keith Miser
Colorado State University

L. Jackson Newell
University of Utah

Steven G. Olswang
University of Washington

Sherry Sayles-Folks
Eastern Michigan University

Karl Schilling
Miami University

Charles Schroeder
University of Missouri

Lawrence A. Sherr
University of Kansas

Patricia A. Spencer
Riverside Community College

Marilla D. Svinicki
University of Texas at Austin

David Sweet
OERI, U.S. Dept. of Education

Barbara E. Taylor
Association of Governing Boards

Kathe Taylor
State of Washington Higher Education Coordinating Board

Donald H. Wulff
University of Washington

Manta Yorke
Liverpool John Moores University

REVIEW PANEL

Charles Adams
University of Massachusetts-Amherst

Louis Albert
American Association for Higher Education

Richard Alfred
University of Michigan

Henry Lee Allen
University of Rochester

Philip G. Altbach
Boston College

Marilyn J. Amey
University of Kansas

Kristine L. Anderson
Florida Atlantic University

Karen D. Arnold
Boston College

Robert J. Barak
Iowa State Board of Regents

Alan Bayer
Virginia Polytechnic Institute and State University

John P. Bean
Indiana University-Bloomington

John M. Braxton
Peabody College, Vanderbilt University

Ellen M. Brier
Tennessee State University

Barbara E. Brittingham
The University of Rhode Island

Dennis Brown
University of Kansas

Peter McE. Buchanan
Council for Advancement and Support of Education

Patricia Carter
University of Michigan

John A. Centra
Syracuse University

Arthur W. Chickering
George Mason University

Darrel A. Clowes
Virginia Polytechnic Institute and State University

Deborah M. DiCroce
Piedmont Virginia Community College

Cynthia S. Dickens
Mississippi State University

Sarah M. Dinham
University of Arizona

Kenneth A. Feldman
State University of New York-Stony Brook

Dorothy E. Finnegan
The College of William & Mary

Mildred Garcia
Montclair State College

Rodolfo Z. Garcia
Commission on Institutions of Higher Education

Kenneth C. Green
University of Southern California

James Hearn
University of Georgia

Edward R. Hines
Illinois State University

Deborah Hunter
University of Vermont

Philo Hutcheson
Georgia State University

Bruce Anthony Jones
University of Pittsburgh

Elizabeth A. Jones
The Pennsylvania State University

Kathryn Kretschmer
University of Kansas

Marsha V. Krotseng
State College and University Systems of West Virginia

George D. Kuh
Indiana University-Bloomington

Daniel T. Layzell
University of Wisconsin System

Patrick G. Love
Kent State University

Cheryl D. Lovell
State Higher Education Executive Officers

Meredith Jane Ludwig
American Association of State Colleges and Universities

Dewayne Matthews
Western Interstate Commission for Higher Education

Mantha V. Mehallis
Florida Atlantic University

Toby Milton
Essex Community College

James R. Mingle
State Higher Education Executive Officers

John A. Muffo
Virginia Polytechnic Institute and State University

L. Jackson Newell
Deep Springs College

James C. Palmer
Illinois State University

Robert A. Rhoads
The Pennsylvania State University

G. Jeremiah Ryan
Harford Community College

Mary Ann Danowitz Sagaria
The Ohio State University

Daryl G. Smith
The Claremont Graduate School

William G. Tierney
University of Southern California

Susan B. Twombly
University of Kansas

Robert A. Walhaus
University of Illinois-Chicago

Harold Wechsler
University of Rochester

Elizabeth J. Whitt
University of Illinois-Chicago

Michael J. Worth
The George Washington University

RECENT TITLES

1995 ASHE-ERIC Higher Education Reports

1. Tenure, Promotion, and Reappointment: Legal and Administrative Implications
   Benjamin Baez and John A. Centra

2. Taking Teaching Seriously: Meeting the Challenge of Instructional Improvement
   Michael B. Paulsen and Kenneth A. Feldman

3. Empowering the Faculty: Mentoring Redirected and Renewed
   Gaye Luna and Deborah L. Cullen

1994 ASHE-ERIC Higher Education Reports

1. The Advisory Committee Advantage: Creating an Effective Strategy for Programmatic Improvement
   Lee Teitel

2. Collaborative Peer Review: The Role of Faculty in Improving College Teaching
   Larry Keig and Michael D. Waggoner

3. Prices, Productivity, and Investment: Assessing Financial Strategies in Higher Education
   Edward P. St. John

4. The Development Officer in Higher Education: Toward an Understanding of the Role
   Michael J. Worth and James W. Asp, II

5. The Promises and Pitfalls of Performance Indicators in Higher Education
   Gerald Gaither, Brian P. Nedwek, and John E. Neal

6. A New Alliance: Continuous Quality and Classroom Effectiveness
   Mimi Wolverton

7. Redesigning Higher Education: Producing Dramatic Gains in Student Learning
   Lion F. Gardiner

8. Student Learning Outside the Classroom: Transcending Artificial Boundaries
   George D. Kuh, Katie Branch Douglas, Jon P. Lund, and Jackie Ramin-Gyurnek

1993 ASHE-ERIC Higher Education Reports

1. The Department Chair: New Roles, Responsibilities, and Challenges
   Alan T. Seagren, John W. Creswell, and Daniel W. Wheeler

2. Sexual Harassment in Higher Education: From Conflict to Community
   Robert O. Riggs, Patricia H. Murrell, and Joann C. Cutting

---

8. Crossing Pedagogical Oceans: International Teaching
   Assistants in U.S. Undergraduate Education
   *Rosslyn M. Smith, Patricia Byrd, Gayle L. Nelson, Ralph
   Pat Barrett, and Janet C. Constantinides*

1991 ASHE-ERIC Higher Education Reports

1. Active Learning: Creating Excitement in the Classroom
   Charles C. Bonwell and James A. Eison

2. Realizing Gender Equality in Higher Education: The Need to
   Integrate Work/Family Issues
   Nancy Hensel

3. Academic Advising for Student Success: A System of Shared
   Responsibility
   Susan H. Frost

4. Cooperative Learning: Increasing College Faculty Instructional
   Productivity
   David W. Johnson, Roger T. Johnson, and Karl A. Smith

5. High School-College Partnerships: Conceptual Models,
   Programs, and Issues
   Arthur Richard Greenberg

6. Meeting the Mandate: Renewing the College and
   Departmental Curriculum
   William Toombs and William Tierney

7. Faculty Collaboration: Enhancing the Quality of Scholarship
   and Teaching
   Ann E. Austin and Roger G. Baldwin

8. Strategies and Consequences: Managing the Costs in Higher
   Education
   John S. Waggaman

1990 ASHE-ERIC Higher Education Reports

1. The Campus Green: Fund Raising in Higher Education
   Barbara E. Brittingham and Thomas R. Pezzullo

2. The Emeritus Professor: Old Rank New Meaning
   James E. Mauch, Jack W. Birch, and Jack Matthews

3. "High Risk" Students in Higher Education: Future Trends
   Dionne J. Jones and Betty Collier Watson

4. Budgeting for Higher Education at the State Level: Enigma,
   Paradox, and Ritual
   Daniel T. Layzell and Jan W. Lyddon

5. Proprietary Schools: Programs, Policies, and Prospects
   John B. Lee and Jamie P. Merisotis

ORDER FORM

Quantity

95-4

Amount

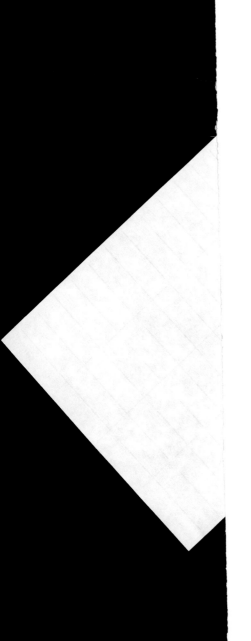

_____ Please begin my subscription to the 1995 *ASHE-ERIC Higher Education Reports* at $98.00, 31% off the cover price, starting with Report 1, 1995. Includes shipping. _____

_____ Please send a complete set of the 1994 *ASHE-ERIC Higher Education Reports* at $98.00, 31% off the cover price. Please add shipping charge below. _____

Individual reports are available at the following prices:
1993, 1994 and 1995, $18.00; 1988-1992, $17.00; 1980-1987, $15.00

SHIPPING CHARGES
For orders of more than 50 books, please call for shipping information.

	1st three books	Ea. addl. book
U.S., 48 Contiguous States		
Ground:	$3.75	$0.15
2nd Day*:	8.25	1.10
Next Day*:	18.00	1.60
Alaska & Hawaii (2nd Day Only)*:	13.25	1.40

U.S. Territories and Foreign Countries: Please call for shipping information.
*Order will be shipped within 24 hours of request.
All prices shown on this form are subject to change.

PLEASE SEND ME THE FOLLOWING REPORTS:

Quantity	Report No.	Year	Title	Amount

Please check one of the following:
☐ Check enclosed, payable to GWU-ERIC.
☐ Purchase order attached ($45.00 minimum).
☐ Charge my credit card indicated below:
   ☐ Visa   ☐ MasterCard

Subtotal:

Shipping:

Total Due:

Expiration Date_____

Name_____

Title_____

Institution_____

Address_____

City _____ State _____ Zip_____

Phone _____ Fax _____Telex_____

Signature _____ Date_____

SEND ALL ORDERS TO: ASHE-ERIC Higher Education Reports
The George Washington University
One Dupont Cir., Ste. 630, Washington, DC 20036-1183
Phone: (202) 296-2597 • Toll-free: 800-773-ERIC

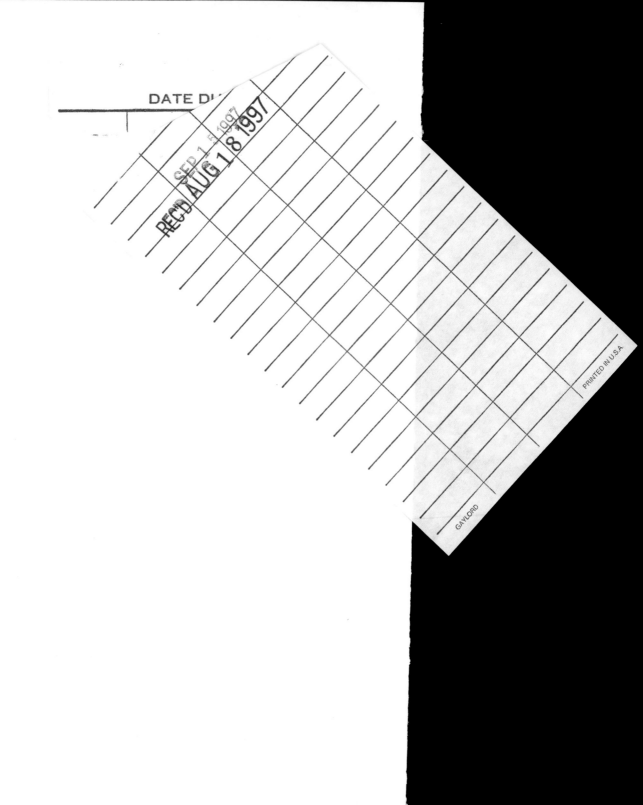